Tiny Luttre

E. W. Hornung

Alpha Editions

This edition published in 2023

ISBN : 9789362093387

Design and Setting By
Alpha Editions
www.alphaedis.com
Email - info@alphaedis.com

Contents

CHAPTER I.
THE COMING OF TINY.

Swift of Wallandoon was visibly distraught. He had driven over to the township in the heat of the afternoon to meet the coach. The coach was just in sight, which meant that it could not arrive for at least half an hour. Yet nothing would induce Swift to wait quietly in the hotel veranda; he paid no sort of attention to the publican who pressed him to do so. The iron roofs of the little township crackled in the sun with a sound as of distant musketry; their sharp-edged shadows lay on the sand like sheets of zinc that might be lifted up in one piece; and a hot wind in full blast played steadily upon Swift's neck and ears. He had pulled up in the shade, and was leaning forward, with his wide-awake tilted over his nose, and his eyes on a cloud of dust between the bellying sand-hills and the dark blue sky. The cloud advanced, revealing from time to time a growing speck. That speck was the coach which Swift had come to meet.

He was a young man with broad shoulders and good arms, and a general air of smartness and alacrity about which there could be no mistake. He had dark hair and a fair mustache; his eye was brown and alert; and much wind and sun had reddened a face that commonly gave the impression of complete capability with a sufficiency of force. This afternoon, however, Swift lacked the confident look of the thoroughly capable young man. And he was even younger than he looked; he was young enough to fancy that the owner of Wallandoon, who was a passenger by the approaching coach, had traveled five hundred miles expressly to deprive John Swift of the fine position to which recent good luck had promoted him.

He could think of nothing else to bring Mr. Luttrell all the way from Melbourne at the time of year when a sheep station causes least anxiety. The month was April, there had been a fair rainfall since Christmas, and only in his last letter Mr. Luttrell had told Swift that all he need do for the present was to take care of the fences and let the sheep take care of themselves. The next news was a telegram to the effect that Mr. Luttrell was coming up country to see for himself how things were going at Wallandoon. Having stepped into the managership by an accident, and even so merely as a trial man, young Swift at once made sure that his trial was at an end. It did not strike him that in spite of his youth he was the ideal person for the post. Yet this was obvious. He had five years' experience of the station he was to manage. The like merit is not often in the market. Swift seemed to forget that. Neither did he take comfort from the fact that Mr. Luttrell was an old friend of his family in Victoria, and hitherto his own highly satisfied employer. Hitherto, or until the last three months, he had not tried to manage

Mr. Luttrell's station. If he had failed in that time to satisfy its owner, then he would at once go elsewhere; but for many things he wished most keenly to stay at Wallandoon; and he was thinking of these things now, while the coach grew before his eyes.

Of his five years on Wallandoon the last two had been infinitely less enjoyable than the three that had gone before. There was a simple reason for the difference. Until two years ago Mr. Luttrell had himself managed the station, and had lived there with his wife and family. That had answered fairly well while the family were young, thanks to a competent governess for the girls. But when the girls grew up it became time to make a change. The squatter was a wealthy man, and he could perfectly well afford the substantial house which he had already built for himself in a Melbourne suburb. The social splashing of his wife and daughters after their long seclusion in the wilderness was also easily within his means, if not entirely to his liking; but he was a mild man married to a weak woman; and he happened to be bent on a little splash on his own account in politics. Choosing out of many applicants the best possible manager for Wallandoon, the squatter presently entered the Victorian legislature, and embraced the new interests so heartily that he was nearly two years in discovering his best possible manager to be both a failure and a fraud.

It was this discovery that had given Swift an opening whose very splendor accounted for his present doubts and fears. Had his chance been spoilt by Herbert Luttrell, who had lately been on Wallandoon as Swift's overseer, for some ten days only, when the two young fellows had failed to pull together? This was not likely, for Herbert at his worst was an honest ruffian, who had taken the whole blame (indeed it was no more than his share) of that fiasco. Swift, however, could think of nothing else; nor was there time; for now the coach was so close that the crack of the driver's whip was plainly heard, and above the cluster of heads on the box a white handkerchief fluttered against the sky.

The publican whom Swift had snubbed addressed another remark to him from the veranda:

"There's a petticoat on board."

"So I see."

The coach came nearer.

"She's your boss's daughter," affirmed the publican—"the best of 'em."

"So you're cracking!"

"Well, wait a minute. What now?"

Swift prolonged the minute. "You're right," he said, hastily tying his reins to the brake.

"I am so."

"Heaven help me!" muttered Swift as he jumped to the ground. "There's nothing ready for her. They might have told one!"

A moment later five heaving horses stood sweating in the sun, and Swift, reaching up his hand, received from a gray-bearded gentleman on the box seat a grip from which his doubts and fears should have died on the spot. If they did, however, it was only to make way for a new and unlooked-for anxiety, for little Miss Luttrell was smiling down at him through a brown gauze veil, as she poked away the handkerchief she had waved, leaving a corner showing against her dark brown jacket; and how she was to be made comfortable at the homestead, all in a minute, Swift did not know.

"She insisted on coming," said Mr. Luttrell, with a smile. "Is it any good her getting down?"

"Can you take me in?" asked the girl.

"We'll do our best," said Swift, holding the ladder for her descent.

Her shoes made a daintier imprint in the sand than it had known for two whole years. She smiled as she gave her hand to Swift; it was small, too, and Swift had not touched a lady's hand for many months. There was very little of her altogether, but the little was entirely pleasing. Embarrassed though he was, Swift was more than pleased to see the young girl again, and her smiles that struggled through the brown gauze like sunshine through a mist. She had not worn gauze veils two years ago; and two years ago she had been content with fare that would scarcely please her to-day, while naturally the living at the station was rougher now than in the days of the ladies. It was all very well for her to smile. She ought never to have come without a word of warning. Swift felt responsible and aggrieved.

He helped Mr. Luttrell to carry their baggage from the coach to the buggy drawn up in the shade. Miss Luttrell went to the horses' heads and stroked their noses; they were Bushman and Brownlock, the old safe pair she had many a time driven herself. In a moment she was bidden to jump up. There had been very little luggage to transfer. The most cumbrous piece was a hamper, of which Swift formed expectations that were speedily confirmed. For Miss Luttrell remarked, pointing to the hamper as she took her seat:

"At least we have brought our own rations; but I am afraid they will make you horribly uncomfortable bchind there?"

Swift was on the back seat. "Not a bit," he answered; "I was much more uncomfortable until I saw the hamper."

"Don't you worry about us, Jack," said Mr. Luttrell as they drove off. "Whatever you do, don't worry about Tiny. Give her travelers' rations and send her to the travelers' hut. That's all she deserves, when she wasn't on the way-bill. She insisted on coming at the last moment; I told her it wasn't fair."

"But it's very jolly," said Swift gallantly.

"It was just like her," Mr. Luttrell chuckled; "she's as unreliable as ever."

The girl had been looking radiantly about her as they drove along the single broad, straggling street of the township. She now turned her head to Swift, and her eyes shot through her veil in a smile. That abominable veil went right over her broad-brimmed hat, and was gathered in and made fast at the neck. Swift could have torn it from her head; he had not seen a lady smile for months. Also, he was beginning to make the astonishing discovery that somehow she was altered, and he was curious to see how much, which was impossible through the gauze.

"Is that true?" he asked her. He had known her for five years.

"I suppose so," she returned carelessly; and immediately her sparkling eyes wandered. "There's old Mackenzie in the post office veranda. He was a detestable old man, but I must wave to him; it's so good to be back!"

"But you own to being unreliable?" persisted Swift.

"I don't know," Miss Luttrell said, tossing the words to him over her shoulder, because her attention was not for the manager. "Is it so very dreadful if I am? What's the good of being reliable? It's much more amusing to take people by surprise. Your face was worth the journey when you saw me on the coach! But you see I haven't surprised Mackenzie; he doesn't look the least impressed; I dare say he thinks it was last week we all went away. I hate him!"

"Here are the police barracks," said Swift, seeing that all her interest was in the old landmarks; "we have a new sergeant since you left."

"If *he's* in *his* veranda I shall shout out to him who I am, and how long I have been away, and how good it is to get back."

"She's quite capable of doing it," Mr. Luttrell chimed in, chuckling afresh; "there's never any knowing what she'll do next."

But the barracks veranda was empty, and it was the last of the township buildings. There was now nothing ahead but the rim of scrub, beyond which, among the sand-hills, sweltered the homestead of Wallandoon.

"I've come back with a nice character, have I not?" the girl now remarked, turning to Swift with another smile.

"You must have earned it; I can quite believe that you have," laughed Swift. He had known her in short dresses.

"Ha! ha! You see he remembers all about you, my dear."

"Do you, Jack?" the girl said.

"Do I not!" said Jack.

And he said no more. He was grateful to her for addressing him, though only once, by his Christian name. He had been intimate with the whole family, and it seemed both sensible and pleasant to resume a friendly footing from the first. He would have called the girl by her Christian name too, only this was so seldom heard among her own people. Tiny she was by nature, and Tiny she had been by name also, from her cradle. Certainly she had been Tiny to Swift two years ago, and already she had called him Jack; but he saw in neither circumstance any reason why she should be Tiny to him still. It was different from a proper name. Her proper name was Christina, but unreliable though she confessedly was, she might perhaps be relied upon to jeer if he came out with that. And he would not call her "Miss Luttrell." He thought about it and grew silent; but this was because his thoughts had glided from the girl's name to the girl herself.

She had surprised him in more ways than one—in so many ways that already he stood almost in awe of the little person whom formerly he had known so well. Christina had changed, as it was only natural that she should have changed; but because we are prone to picture our friends as last we saw them, no matter how long ago, not less natural was Swift's surprise. It was unreasoning, however, and not the kind of surprise to last. In a few minutes his wonder was that Christina had changed so little. To look at her she had scarcely changed at all. A certain finality of line was perceptible in the figure, but if anything she was thinner than of old. As for her face, what he could see of it through the maddening gauze was the face of Swift's memory. Her voice was a little different; in it was a ring of curiously deliberate irony, charming at first as a mere affectation. A more noteworthy alteration had taken place in her manner: she had acquired the manner of a finished young woman of the world and of society. Already she had shown that she could become considerably excited without forfeiting any of the grace and graciousness and self-possession that were now conspicuously hers; and before the homestead was reached she exhibited such a saintly sweetness in repose as only enhanced the lambent deviltry playing about most of her looks and tones. If Swift was touched with awe in her presence, that can hardly be wondered at in one who went for months together without setting eyes upon a lady.

The drive was a long one—so long that when they sighted the homestead it came between them and the setting sun. The main building with its long, regular roof lay against the red sky like some monstrous ingot. The hot wind had fallen, and the station pines stood motionless, drawn in ink. As they drove through the last gate they could hear the dogs barking; and Christina distinguished the voice of her own old short-haired collie, which she had bequeathed to Swift, who was repaid for the sound with a final smile. He hardly knew why, but this look made the girl's old self live to him as neither look nor word had done yet, though her face was turned away from the light, and the stupid veil still fell before it.

But the less fascinating side of her arrival was presently engaging his attention. He hastily interviewed Mrs. Duncan, an elderly godsend new to the place since the Luttrells had left it, and never so invaluable as now. Into Mrs. Duncan's hands Christina willingly submitted herself, for she was really tired out. Swift did not see her again until supper, which afforded further proofs of Mrs. Duncan's merits in a time of need. Meanwhile, Mr. Luttrell had finally disabused him of the foolish fears he had entertained while waiting for the coach. Swift's youth, which has shown itself in these fears, comes out also in the ease with which he now forgot them. They had made him unhappy for three whole days; yet he dared to feel indignant because his owner, who had confirmed his command instead of dismissing him from it, chose to talk sheep at the supper table. Swift seemed burning to hear of the eldest Miss Luttrell, who was Miss Luttrell no longer, having married a globe-trotting Londoner during her first season and gone home. He asked Christina several questions about Ruth (whose other name he kept forgetting) and her husband. But Mr. Luttrell lost no chance of rounding up the conversation and yarding it in the sheep pens; and Swift had the ingratitude to resent this. Still more did he resent the hour he was forced to spend in the store after supper, examining the books and discussing recent results and future plans with Mr. Luttrell, while his subordinate, the storekeeper, enjoyed the society of Christina. The business in the store was not only absurdly premature and irksome in itself, but it made it perfectly impossible for Swift to hear any more that night of the late Ruth Luttrell, whose present name was not to be remembered. He found it hard to possess his soul in patience and to answer questions satisfactorily under such circumstances. For an hour, indeed, he did both; but the station store faced the main building, and when Tiny Luttrell appeared in the veranda of the latter with a lighted candle in her hand, he could do neither any longer. Saying candidly that he must bid her good-night, he hurried out of the store and across the yard, and was in time to catch Christina at one end of the broad veranda which entirely surrounded the house.

At supper Mr. Luttrell had made him take the head of the table, by virtue of his office, declaring that he himself was merely a visitor. And on the strength of that Swift was perhaps justified now in adding a host's apology to his good-night. "I'm afraid you'll have to rough it most awfully," was what he said.

"Far from it. You have given me my old room, the one we papered with *Australasians*, if you remember; they are only a little more fly-blown than they used to be."

This was Christina's reply, which naturally led to more.

"But it won't be as comfortable as it used to be," said Swift unhappily; "and it won't be what you are accustomed to nowadays."

"Never mind, it's the dearest little den in the colonies!"

"That sounds as if you were glad to get back to Riverina?"

"Glad? No one knows how glad I am."

One person knew now. The measure of her gladness was expressed in her face not less than in her tones, and it was no ordinary measure. Over the candle she held in her hand Swift was enabled for the first time to peer unobstructedly into her face. He found it more winsome than ever, but he noticed some ancient blemishes under the memorable eyes. She had, in fact, some freckles, which he recognized with the keenest joy. She might stoop to a veil—she had not sunk to doctoring her complexion; she had come back to the bush an incomplete worldling after all. Yet there was that in her face which made him feel a stranger to her still.

"Do you know," he said, smiling, "that I'm in a great funk of you? I can't say quite what it is, but somehow you're so grand. I suppose it's Melbourne."

Miss Luttrell thanked him, bowing so low that her candle shed grease upon the boards. "You've altered too," she added in his own manner; "I suppose it's being boss. But I haven't seen enough of you to be sure. You evidently told off your new storekeeper to entertain me for the evening. He is a trying young man; he *will* talk. But of course he is a new chum fresh from home."

"Still he's a very good little chap; but it wasn't my fault that he and I didn't change places. Mr. Luttrell wanted to speak to me about several things, besides glancing through the books; I thought we might have put it off, and I wondered how you were getting on. By the way, it struck me once or twice that your father was coming up to give me the sack; and it's just the reverse, for now I'm permanent manager."

He told her this with a natural exultation, but she did not seem impressed by it. "Do you know why he did come up?" she asked him.

"Yes; for his Easter holidays, chiefly."

"And why I would come with him?"

"No; I'm afraid we never mentioned you. I suppose you came for a holiday too?"

"Shall I tell you why I did come?"

"I wish you would."

"Well, I came to say good-by to Wallandoon," said Christina solemnly.

"You're going to be married!" exclaimed Swift, with conviction, but with perfect nonchalance.

"Not if I know it," cried Christina. "Are you?"

"Not I."

"But there's Miss Trevor of Meringul!"

"I see them once in six months."

"That may be in the bond."

"Well, never mind Miss Trevor of Meringul. You haven't told me how it is you've come to say good-by to the station, Miss Luttrell of Wallandoon."

"Then I'll tell you, seriously: it's because I sail for England on the 4th of May."

"For England!"

"Yes, and I'm not at all keen about it, I can tell you. But I'm not going to see England, I'm going to see Ruth; Australia's worth fifty Englands any day."

Swift had recovered from his astonishment. "I don't know," he said doubtfully; "most of us would like a trip home, you know, just to see what the old country's like; though I dare say it isn't all it's cracked up to be."

"Of course it isn't. I hate it!"

"But if you've never been there?"

"I judge from the people—from the samples they send out. Your new storekeeper is one; you meet worse down in Melbourne. Herbert's going with me; he's going to Cambridge, if they'll have him. Didn't you know that? But he could go alone, and if it wasn't for Ruth I wouldn't cross Hobson's Bay to see their old England!"

The serious bitterness of her tone struck him afterward as nothing less than grotesque; but at the moment he was gazing into her face, thoughtfully yet without thoughts.

"It's good for Herbert," he said presently. "I couldn't do anything with him here; he offered to fight me when I tried to make him work. I suppose he will be three or four years at Cambridge; but how long are you going to stay with Mrs.—Mrs. Ruth?"

"How stupid you are at remembering a simple name! Do try to remember that her name is Holland. I beg your pardon, Jack, but you have been really very forgetful this evening. I think it must be Miss Trevor of Meringul."

"It isn't. I'm very sorry. But you haven't told me how long you think of staying at home."

"How long?" said the young girl lightly. "It may be for years and years, and it may be forever and ever!"

He looked at her strangely, and she darted out her hand.

"Good-night again, Jack."

"Good-night again."

What with the pauses, each of them an excellent opportunity for Christina to depart, it had taken them some ten minutes to say that which ought not to have lasted one. But you must know that this was nothing to their last good-night, on the self-same spot two years before, when she had rested in his arms.

CHAPTER II.
SWIFT OF WALLANDOON.

Christina was awakened in the morning by the holland blind flapping against her open window. It was a soft, insinuating sound, that awoke one gradually, and to Christina both the cause and the awakening itself seemed incredibly familiar. So had she lain and listened in the past, as each day broke in her brain. When she opened her eyes the shadow of the sash wriggled on the blind as it flapped, a blade of sunshine lay under the door that opened upon the veranda, and neither sight was new to her. The same sheets of the *Australasian* with which her own hands had once lined the room, for want of a conventional wallpaper, lined it still; the same area of printed matter was in focus from the pillow, and she actually remembered an advertisement that caught her eye. It used to catch her eye two years before. Thus it became difficult to believe in those two years; and it was very pleasant to disbelieve in them. More than pleasant Christina found it to lie where she was, hearing the old noises (the horses were run up before she rose), seeing the old things, and dreaming that the last two years were themselves a dream. Her life as it stood was a much less charming composition than several possible arrangements of the same material, impossible now. This is not strange, but it was a little strange that neither sweet impossibilities nor bitter actualities fascinated her much; for so many good girls are morbidly introspective. As for Christina, let it be clearly and early understood that she was neither an introspective girl by nature nor a particularly good one from any point of view. She was not in the habit of looking back; but to look back on the old days here at the station without thinking of later days was like reading an uneven book for the second time, leaving out the poor part.

In making, but still more in closing that gap in her life (as you close a table after taking out a leaf) she was immensely helped by the associations of the present moment. They breathed of the remote past only; their breath was sweet and invigorating. Her affection for Wallandoon was no affectation; she loved it as she loved no other place. And if, as she dressed, her thoughts dwelt more on the young manager of the station than on the station itself, that only illustrates the difference between an association and an associate. There is human interest in the one, but it does not follow that Tiny Luttrell was immoderately interested in Jack Swift. Even to herself she denied that she had ever done more than like him very much. To some "nonsense" in the past she was ready to own. But in the vocabulary of a Tiny Luttrell a little "nonsense" may cover a calendar of mild crimes. It is only the Jack Swifts who treat the nonsense seriously and deny that the crimes are anything of the sort, because for their part they "mean it." Women are not deceived. Besides, it is less shame for them to say they never meant it.

"He must marry Flo Trevor of Meringul," Christina said aloud. "It's what we all expect of him. It's his duty. But she isn't pretty, poor thing!"

The remarks happened to be made to Christina's own reflection in the glass. She, as we know, was very pretty indeed. Her small head was finely turned, and carried with her own natural grace. Her hair was of so dark a brown as to be nearly black, but there was not enough of it to hide the charming contour of her head. If she could have had the altering of one feature, she would probably have shortened her lips; but their red freshness justified their length; and the crux of a woman's beauty, her nose, happened to be Christina's best point. Her eyes were a sweeter one. Their depth of blue is seen only under dark blue skies, and they seemed the darker for her hair. But with all her good features, because she was not an English girl, but an Australian born and bred, she had no complexion to speak of, being pale and slightly freckled. Yet no one held that those blemishes prevented her from being pretty; while some maintained that they did not even detract from her good looks, and a few that they saved her from perfection and were a part of her charm. The chances are that the authorities quoted were themselves her admirers one and all. She had many such. To most of them her character had the same charm as her face; it, too, was freckled with faults for which they loved her the more.

One of the many she met presently, but one of them now, though in his day the first of all. Swift was hastening along the veranda as she issued forth, a consciously captivating figure in her clean white frock. He had on his wide-awake, a newly filled water-bag dripped as he carried it, the drops drying under their eyes in the sun, and Christina foresaw at once his absence for the day. She was disappointed, perhaps because he was one of the many; certainly it was for this reason she did not let him see her disappointment. He told her that he was going with her father to the out-station. That was fourteen miles away. It meant a lonely day for Christina at the homestead. So she said that a lonely day there was just what she wanted, to overhaul the dear old place all by herself, and to revel in it like a child without feeling that she was being watched. But she told a franker story some hours later, when Swift found her still on the veranda where he had left her, but this was now the shady side, seated in a wicker chair and frowning at a book. For she promptly flung away that crutch of her solitude, and seemed really glad to see him. Her look made him tingle. He sat down on the edge of the veranda and leaned his back against a post. Then he inquired, rather diffidently, how the day had gone with Miss Luttrell.

"I am ashamed to tell you," said Christina graciously, for though his diffidence irritated her, she was quite as glad to see him as she looked, "that I have been bored very nearly to death!"

"I knew you would be," Swift said quite bitterly; but his bitterness was against an absent man, who had gone indoors to rest.

"I don't see how you could know anything," remarked Christina. "I certainly didn't know it myself; and I'm very much ashamed of it, that's another thing! I love every stick about the place. But I never knew a hotter morning; the sand in the yard was like powdered cinders, and you can't go poking about very long when everything you touch is red hot. Then one felt tired. Mrs. Duncan took pity on me and came and talked to me; she must be an acquisition to you, I am sure; but her cooking's better than her conversation. I think she must have sent the new chum to me to take her place; anyway I've had a dose of him, too, I can tell you!"

"Oh, he's been cutting his work, has he?"

"He has been doing the civil; I think he considered that his work."

"And quite right too! Tell me, what do you think of him?"

Christina made a grotesque grimace. "He's such a little Englishman," she simply said.

"Well, he can't help that, you know," said Swift, laughing; "and he's not half a bad little chap, as I told you last night."

"Oh, not a bit bad; only typical. He has told me his history. It seems he missed the army at home, front door and back, in spite of his crammer—I mean his cwammer. He was no use, so they sent him out to us."

"And he is gradually becoming of some use to us, or rather to me; he really is," protested Swift in the interests of fair play, which a man loves. "You laugh, but I like the fellow. He's much more use—forgive my saying so—than Herbert ever would have been—here. At all events he doesn't want to fight! He's willing, I will say that for him. And I think it was rather nice of him to tell you about himself."

"It's nicer of you to think so," said Christina to herself. And her glance softened so that he noticed the difference, for he was becoming sensitive to a slight but constant hardness of eye and tongue distressing to find in one's divinity.

"He went so far as to hint at an affair of the heart," she said aloud, and he saw her eyes turn hard again, so that his own glanced off them and fell. But he forced a chuckle as he looked down.

"Well, you gave him your sympathy there, I hope?"

"Not I, indeed. I urged him to forget all about her; she has forgotten all about him long before now, you may be sure. He only thinks about her still because it's pleasant to have somebody to think about at a lonely place like this; and if she's thinking about him it's because he's away in the wilderness and there's a glamour about that. It wouldn't prevent her marrying another man to-morrow, and it won't prevent him making up to some other girl when he gets the chance."

"So that's your experience, is it?"

"Never mind whose experience it is. I advised the young man to give up thinking about the young woman, that's all, and it's my advice to every young man situated as he is."

Swift was not amused. Yet he refused to believe that her advice was intended for himself: firstly, because it was so coolly given, which was his ignorance, and secondly, because, literally speaking, he was not himself situated as the young Englishman was, which was merely unimaginative. In his determination, however, not to meet her in generalizations, but to get back to the storekeeper, he was wise enough.

"I know something about his affairs, too," he said quietly; "he's the frankest little fellow in the world; and I have given him very different advice, I must say."

Tiny Luttrell bent down on him a gaze of fiendish innocence.

"And what sort of advice does he give you, pray?"

"You had better ask him," said Swift feebly, but with effect, for he was honestly annoyed, and man enough to show it. As he spoke, indeed, he rose.

"What, are you going?"

"Yes; you go in for being too hard altogether."

"I don't go in for it. I am hard. I'm as hard as nails," said Christina rapidly.

"So I see," he said, and another weak return was strengthened by his firmness; for he was going away as he spoke, and he never looked round.

"I wouldn't lose my temper," she called after him.

Her face was white. He disappeared. She colored angrily.

"Now I hate you," she whispered to herself; but she probably respected him more, and that was as it only should have been long ago.

But Swift was in an awkward position, which indeed he deserved for the unsuspected passages that had once taken place between Tiny Luttrell and himself. It is true that those passages had occurred at the very end of the Luttrells' residence at Wallandoon; they had not been going on for a period preceding the end; but there is no denying that they were reprehensible in themselves, and pardonable only on the plea of exceeding earnestness. Swift would not have made that excuse for himself, for he felt it to be a poor one, though of his own sincerity he was and had been unwaveringly sure. Beyond all doubt he was properly in love, and, being so, it was not until the girl stopped writing to him that he honestly repented the lengths to which he had been encouraged to go. It is easy to be blameless through the post, but they had kept up their perfectly blameless correspondence for a very few weeks when Christina ceased firing; she was to have gone on forever. He was just persistent enough to make it evident that her silence was intentional; then the silence became complete, and it was never again broken. For if Swift's self-control was limited, his self-respect was considerable, and this made him duly regret the limitations of his self-control. His boy's soul bled with a boy's generous regrets. He had kissed her, of course, and I wonder whose fault you think that was? I know which of them regretted and which forgot it. The man would have given one of his fingers to have undone those kisses, that made him think less of himself and less of his darling. Nothing could make him love her less. He heard no more of her, but that made no difference. And now they were together again, and she was hard, and it made this difference: that he wanted her worse than ever, and for her own gain now as much as for his.

But two years had altered him also. In a manner he too was hardened; but he was simply a stronger, not a colder man. The muscles of his mind were set; his soul was now as sinewy as his body. He knew what he wanted, and what would not do for him instead. He wanted a great deal, but he meant having it or nothing. This time she should give him her heart before he took her hand; he swore it through his teeth; and you will realize how he must have known her of old even to have thought it. The curious thing is that, having shown him what she was, she should have made him love her as he did. But that was Tiny Luttrell.

She was half witch, half coquette, and her superficial cynicism was but a new form of her coquetry. He liked it less than the unsophisticated methods of the old days. Indeed, he liked the girl less, while loving her more. She had given him the jar direct in one conversation, but even on indifferent subjects she spoke with a bitterness which he thoroughly disliked; while some of her prejudices he could not help thinking irredeemably absurd. As a shrill decrier of England, for instance, she may have amused him, but he hardly admired her in that character. In a word, he thought her, and rightly, a good deal spoilt by her town life; but he hated towns, and it was a proof of her worth in his eyes that she was not hopelessly spoilt. He saw hope for her still—if she would marry him. He was a modest man in general, but he did feel this most strongly. She was going to England without caring whether she went or not; she would do much better by marrying him and coming back to her old home in the bush. That home she loved, whether she loved him or not; in it she had grown up simple and credulous and sweet, with a wicked side that only picked out her sweetness; in it he believed that her life and his might yet be beautiful. The feeling made him sometimes rejoice that she had fallen a little out of love with her life, so that he might show her with all the effect of contrast what life and love really were; it thrilled his heart with generous throbs, it brought the moisture to his honest eyes, and it came to him oftener and with growing force as the days went on, by reason of certain signs they brought forth in Christiana. Her voice lost its bitterness in his ears, not because he had grown used to notes that had jarred him in the beginning, but because the discordant strings came gradually into tune. Her freshness came back to her with the charm and influence of the wilderness she loved; her old self lived again to Jack Swift. On the other hand, she came to realize her own delight in the old good life as she had never realized it before; she felt that henceforward she should miss it as she had not missed it yet. Now she could have defined her sensations and given reasons for them. She spent many hours in the saddle, on a former mount of hers that Swift had run up for her; often he rode with her, and the scent of the pines, the swelling of the sand-hills against the sky, the sense of Nothing between the horses' ears and the sunset, spoke to her spirit as they had never done of old. And even so on their rides would she speak to Swift, who listened grimly, hardly daring to answer her for the fear of saying at the wrong moment what he had resolved to say once and for all before she went.

And he chose the wrong moment after all. It was the eve of her going, and they were riding together for the last time; he felt that it was also his last opportunity. So in six miles he made as many remarks, then turned in his saddle and spoke out with overpowering fervor. This may be expected of the self-contained suitor, with whom it is only a question of time, and the longer the time the stronger the outburst. But Christina was not carried away, for she did not quite love him, and the opportunity was a bad one, and Swift's honest method had not improved it. She listened kindly, with her eyes on the distant timbers of the eight-mile whim; but her kindness was fatally calm; and when he waited she refused him firmly. She confessed to a fondness for him. She ascribed this to the years they had known each other. Once and for all she did not love him.

"Not now!" exclaimed the young fellow eagerly. "But you did once! You will again!"

"I never loved you," said the girl gravely. "If you're thinking of two years ago, that was mere nonsense. I don't believe its love with you either, if you only knew it."

"But I do know what it is with me, Tiny! I loved you before you went away, and all the time you were gone. Since you have been back, during these few days, I have got to love you more than ever. And so I shall go on, whatever happens. I can't help it, darling."

Neither could he help saying this; for the hour found him unable to accept his fate quite as he had meant to accept it. Her kindness had something to do with that. And now she spoke more kindly than before.

"Are you sure?" she said.

"Am I sure!" he echoed bitterly.

"It is so easy to deceive oneself."

"I am not deceived."

"It is so easy to imagine yourself——"

"I am not imagining!" cried Swift impatiently. "I am the man who has loved you always, and never any girl but you. If you can't believe that, you must have had a very poor experience of men, Tiny!"

For a moment she looked away from the whim which they were slowly nearing, and her eyes met his.

"I have," she admitted frankly; "I have had a particularly poor experience of them. Yet I am sorry to find you so different from the rest; I can't tell you how sorry I am to find you true to me."

"Sorry?" he said tenderly; for her voice was full of pain, and he could not bear that. "Why should you be sorry, dear?"

"Why—because I never dreamt of being true to you."

For some reason her face flamed as he watched it. There was a pause. Then he said:

"You are not engaged; are you in love?"

"Very far from it."

"Then why mind? If there is no one else you care for you shall care for me yet. I'll make you. I'll wait for you. You don't know me! I won't give you up until you are some other fellow's wife."

His stern eyes, the way his mouth shut on the words, and the manly determination of the words themselves gave the girl a thrill of pleasure and of pride; but also a pang; for at that moment she felt the wish to love him alongside the inability, and all at once she was as sorry for herself as for him.

"What should you mind?" repeated Swift.

"I can't tell you, but you can guess what I have been."

"A flirt?" He laughed aloud. "Darling, I don't care two figs for your flirtations! I wanted you to enjoy yourself. What does it matter how you've enjoyed yourself, so long as you haven't absolutely been getting engaged or falling in love?"

Her chin drooped into her loose white blouse. "I did fall in love," she said slowly—"at any rate I thought so; and I very nearly got engaged."

Swift had never seen so much color in her face.

Presently he said, "What happened?" but immediately added, "I beg your pardon; of course I have no business to ask." His tone was more stiff than strained.

"You *have* business," she answered eagerly, fearful of making him less than friend. "I wouldn't mind telling you the whole thing, except the man's name. And yet," she added rather wistfully, "I suppose you're the only friend I have that doesn't know! It's hard lines to have to tell you."

"Then I don't want to know anything at all about it," exclaimed Swift impulsively. "I would rather you didn't tell me a word, if you don't mind. I am only too thankful to think you got out of it, whatever it was."

"I didn't get out of it."

"You don't—mean—that the man did?"

Swift was aghast.

"I do."

He did not speak, but she heard him breathing. Stealing a look at him, her eyes fell first upon the clenched fist lying on his knee.

She made haste to defend the man.

"It wasn't all his fault; of that I feel sure. If you knew who he was you wouldn't blame him anymore than I do. He was quite a boy, too; I don't suppose he was a free agent. In any case it is all quite, quite over."

"Is it? He was from England—that's why you hate the home people so!"

"Yes, he was from home. He went back very suddenly. It wasn't his fault. He was sent for. But he might have said good-by!"

She spoke reflectively, gazing once more at the whim. They were near it now. The framework cut the sky like some uncouth hieroglyph. To Swift henceforward, on all his lonely journeys hither, it was the emblem of humiliation. But it was not his own humiliation that moistened his clenched hand now.

"I wish I had him here," he muttered.

"Ah! you know nothing about him, you see; I know enough to forgive him. And I have got over it, quite; but the worst of it is that I can't believe any more in any of you—I simply can't."

"Not in me?" asked Swift warmly, for her belief in him, at least, he knew he deserved. "I have always been the same. I have never thought of any other girl but you, and I never will. I love you, darling!"

"After this, Jack?"

He seemed to disappoint her.

"After the same thing if it happens all over again in England! There is no merit in it; I simply can't help myself. While you are away I will wait for you and work for you; only come back free, and I will win you, too, in the end. You are happier here than anywhere else, but you don't know what it is to be really happy as I should make you. Remember that—and this: that I will never give you up until someone else has got you! Now call me conceited or anything you like. I have done bothering you."

"I can only call you foolish," said the girl, though gently. "You are far too good for me. As for conceit, you haven't enough of it, or you would never give me another thought. I still hope you will quite give up thinking about me, and—and try to get over it. But nothing is going to happen in England, I can promise you that much. And I only wish I could get out of going."

He had already shown her how she might get out of it; he was not going to show her afresh or more explicitly, in spite of the temptation to do so. Even to a proud spirit it is difficult to take No when the voice that says it is kind and sorrowful and all but loving. Swift found it easier to bide by his own statement that he had done bothering her; such was his pride.

But he had chosen the wrong moment, and though he had shown less pride than he had meant to show, he was still too proud to improve the right one when it came. He was too proud, indeed, to stand much chance of immediate success in love. Otherwise he might have reminded her with more force and particularity of their former relations; and playing like that he might have won, but he would rather have lost. Perhaps he did not recognize the right moment as such when it fell; but at least he must have seen that it was better than the one he had chosen. It fell in the evening, when Christina's mood became conspicuously sentimental; but Swift happened to be one of the last young men in the world to take advantage of any mere mood.

As on the first evening, Mr. Luttrell was busy in the store, but this time with the storekeeper, who was making out a list of things to be sent up in the drays from Melbourne. Tiny and the manager were thrown together for the last time. She offered to sing a song, and he thanked her gratefully enough. But he listened to her plaintive songs from a far corner of the room, though the room was lighted only by the moonbeams; and when she rose he declared that she was tired and begged her not to sing any more. She could have beaten him for that.

But in leaving the room they lingered on the threshold, being struck by the beauty of the night. The full moon ribbed the station yard with the shadows of the pines, a soft light was burning in the store, and all was so still that the champing of the night-horse in the yard came plainly to their ears, with the chirping of the everlasting crickets. Christina raised her face to Swift; her eyes were wet in the moonlight; there was even a slight tremor of the red lips; and one hand hung down invitingly at her side. She did not love him, but she was beginning to wish that she could love him; and she did love the place. Had he taken that one hand then the chances are he might have kept it. But even Swift never dreamt that this was so. And after that moment it was not so any more. She turned cold, and was cold to the end. Her last words from the top of the coach fell as harshly on a loving ear as any that had preceded them by a week.

"Why need you remind me I am going to England? Enjoy myself! I shall detest the whole thing."

Her last look matched the words.

CHAPTER III.
THE TAIL OF THE SEASON.

"What do you say to sitting it out? The rooms are most awfully crowded, and you dance too well for one; besides, one's anxious to hear your impressions of a London ball."

"One must wait till the ball is over. So far I can't deny that I'm enjoying myself in spite of the crush. But I should rather like to sit out for once, though you needn't be sarcastic about my dancing."

"Well, then, where's a good place?"

"There's a famous corner in the conservatory; it should be empty now that a dance is just beginning."

It was. So it became occupied next moment by Tiny Luttrell and her partner, who allowed that the dimly illumined recess among the tree-ferns deserved its fame. Tiny's partner, however, was only her brother-in-law, Mr. Erskine Holland.

The Luttrells had been exactly a fortnight in England. It was in the earliest hour of the month of July that Christina sat out with her brother-in-law at her first London party; and if she had spent that fortnight chiefly in visiting dressmakers and waiting for results, she had at least found time to get to know Erskine Holland very much better than she had ever done in Melbourne. There she had seen very little of him, partly through being away from home when he first called with an introduction to the family, but more by reason of the short hurdle race he had made of his courtship, marriage, and return to England with his bride. He had taken the matrimonial fences as only an old bachelor can who has been given up as such by his friends. Mr. Holland, though still nearer thirty than forty, had been regarded as a confirmed bachelor when starting on a long sea voyage for the restoration of his health after an autumnal typhoid. His friends were soon to know what weakened health and Australian women can do between them. They beheld their bachelor return within four months, a comfortably married man, with a pleasant little wife who was very fond of him, and in no way jealous of his old friends. That was Mrs. Erskine's great merit, and the secret of the signal success with which she presided over his table in West Kensington, when Erskine had settled down there and returned with steadiness to the good, safe business to which he had been virtually born a partner. For his part, without being enslaved to a degree embarrassing to their friends, Holland made an obviously satisfactory husband. He was good-natured and never exacting; he was well off and generous. One of a wealthy, many-membered firm driving a versatile trade in the East, he was as free personally from business anxieties as was the hall porter at the firm's offices in Lombard Street. There Erskine was the most popular and least useful fraction of the firm, being just a big, fair, genial fellow, fond of laughter and chaff and lawn tennis, and fonder of books than of the newspapers—an eccentric preference in a business man. But as a business man the older partners shook their heads about him. Once as a youngster he had spent a year or two in Lisbon, learning the language and the ropes there, the firm having certain minor interests planted in Portuguese soil on both sides of the Indian Ocean; and those interests just suited Erskine Holland, who had the handling of them, though the older partners nursed their own distrust of a man who boasted of taking his work out of his head each evening when he hung up his office coat. At home Erskine was a man who read more than one guessed, and had his own ideas on a good many subjects. He found his sister-in-law lamentably ignorant, but quite eager to improve her mind at his direction; and this is ever delightful to the man who reads. Also he found her amusing, and that experience was mutual.

A Londoner himself, with many reputable relatives in the town, who rejoiced in the bachelor's marriage and were able to like his wife, he was in a position to gratify to a considerable extent Mrs. Erskine's social desires. That he did so somewhat against his own inclination (much as in Melbourne his father-in-law had done before him) was due to an acutely fair mind allied with a thoroughly kind and sympathetic nature. His own attitude toward society was not free from that slight intellectual superiority which some of the best fellows in the world cannot help; but at least it was perfectly genuine. He treated society as he treated champagne, which he seldom touched, but about which he was curiously fastidious on those chance occasions. He cared as little for the one as for the other, but found the drier brands inoffensive in both cases. The ball to-night was at Lady Almeric's.

"Not a bad corner," Erskine said as he made himself comfortable; "but I'm afraid it's rather thrown away upon me, you know."

"Far from it. I wish I had been dancing with you the whole evening, Erskine," said Christina seriously.

"That's rather obsequious of you. May I ask why?"

"Because I don't think much of my partners so far, to talk to."

"Ha! I knew there was something you wouldn't think much of," cried Erskine Holland. "Have they nothing to say for themselves, then?"

"Oh, plenty. They discover where I come from; then they show their ignorance. They want to know if there is any chance for a fellow on the gold fields now; they have heard of a place called Ballarat, but they aren't certain whether it's a part of Melbourne or nearer Sydney. One man knows some people at Hobart Town, in New Zealand, he fancies. I never knew anything like their ignorance of the colonies!"

Mr. Holland tugged a smile out of his mustache. "Can you tell me how to address a letter to Montreal—is it Quebec or Ontario?" he asked her, as if interested and anxious to learn.

"Goodness knows," replied Christina innocently.

"Then that's rather like their ignorance of the colonies, isn't it? There's not much difference between a group of colonies and a dominion, you see. I'm afraid your partners are not the only people whose geography has been sadly neglected."

Christina laughed.

"My education's been neglected altogether, if it comes to that. As you're taking me in hand, perhaps you'll lend me a geography, as well as Ruskin and Thackeray. Nevertheless, Australia's more important than Canada, you may say what you like, Erskine; and your being smart won't improve my partners."

"Oh! but I thought it was only their conversation?"

"You force me to tell you that their idea of dancing seems limited to pushing you up one side of the room, and dragging you after them down the other. Sometimes they turn you round. Then they're proud of themselves. They never do it twice running."

"That's because there are so many here."

"There are far too many here—that's what's the matter! And I'm a nice person to tell you so," added Tiny penitently, "when it's you and Ruth who have brought me here. But you know I don't mean that I'm not enjoying it, Erskine; I'm enjoying it immensely, and I'm very proud of myself for being here at all. I can't quite explain myself—I don't much like trying to—but there's a something about everything that makes it seem better than anything of the kind that we can do in Melbourne. The music is so splendid, and the floor, and the flowers. I never saw such a few diamonds—or such beauties! Even the ices are the best I ever tasted, and they aren't too sweet. There's something subdued and superior about the whole concern; but it's too subdued; it needs go and swing nearly as badly as it needs elbow-room—of more kinds than one! I'm thinking less of the crowd of people than of their etiquette and ceremony, which hamper you far more. But it's your old England in a nutshell, this ball is: it fits too tight."

"Upon my word," said Erskine, laughing, "I don't think it's at all bad for you to find the old country a tight fit! I'm obliged to you for the expression, Tiny. I only hope it isn't suggested by personal suffering. I have been thinking that you must have a good word to say for our dressmakers, if not for our dancing men."

Christina slid her eyes over the snow and ice of the shimmering attire that had been made for her in haste since her arrival.

"I'm glad you like me," she said, smiling honestly. "I must own I rather like myself in this lot. I didn't want to disgrace you among your fine friends, you see."

"They're more fine than friends, my dear girl. Lady Almeric's the only friend. She has been very nice to Ruth. Most of the people here are rather classy, I can assure you."

He named the flower of the company in a lowered voice. Christina knew one of the names.

"Lady Mary Dromard, did you say?" said she, playing idly with her fan.

"Yes; do you know her?"

"No, but her brother was in Melbourne once as aid-de-camp to the governor. I knew him."

"Ah, that was Lord Manister; he wasn't out there when I was."

"No, he must have come just after you had gone. He only remained a few months, you know. He was a quiet young man with a mania for cricket; we liked him because he set our young men their fashions and yet never gave himself airs. I wonder if he's here as well?"

"I don't think so. I know him by sight, but I haven't seen him. I'm glad to hear he didn't give himself airs; you couldn't say the same for the sister who is here, though I only know her by sight, too."

"He was quite a nice young man," said Christina, shutting up her fan; and as she spoke the music, whose strains had reached them all the time, came to its natural end.

The conservatory suffered instant invasion, Christina and Mr. Holland being afforded the entertainment of disappointing couple after couple who came straight to their corner.

"We're in a coveted spot," whispered Erskine; and his sister-in-law reminded him who had shown the way to it. It was less secluded than remote, so the present occupiers found further entertainment as mere spectators. The same little things amused them both; this was one reason why they got on so well together. They were amused by such trifles as a distant prospect of Ruth, who was innocently enjoying herself at the other end of the conservatory, unaware of their eyes. Erskine might have felt proud, and no doubt he did, for many people considered Ruth even prettier than Christina, with whom, however, they were apt to confuse her, though Holland himself could never see the likeness. He now sat watching his wife in the distance while talking to her sister at his side until a new partner pounced upon Ruth, and bore her away as the music began afresh.

"There goes my chaperon," remarked Christina resignedly.

"Who's your partner now? I'm sorry to say I see mine within ten yards of me," whispered Erskine in some anxiety.

Tiny consulted her card. "It's Herbert," she said.

"Herbert!" said Mr. Holland dubiously. "I'm afraid Herbert's going it; he's deeply employed with a girl in red—I think an American. Shall I take you to Lady Almeric?" His eyes shifted uneasily toward his expectant partner.

"No, I'll wait here for Herbert. Mayn't I? Then I'm going to. You're sure to see him, and you can send him at once. Don't blame Ruth. What does it matter? It will matter if you don't go this instant to your partner; I see it in her eye!"

He left her reluctantly, with the undertaking that Herbert should be at her side in two minutes. But that was rash. Christina soon had the conservatory entirely to herself, whereupon she came out of her corner, so that her brother might find her the more readily. Still he kept her waiting, and she might as well have been lonely in the corner. It was too bad of Herbert to leave her standing there, where she had no business to be by herself, and the music and the throbbing of the floor within a few yards of her. These awkward minutes naturally began to disturb her. They checked and cooled her in the full blast of healthy excitement, and that was bad; they threw her back upon herself straight from her lightest mood, and this was worse. She became abnormally aware of her own presence as she stood looking down and impatiently tapping with her little white slipper upon the marble flags. Even about these there was the grand air which Christina relished; she might have seen her face far below, as though she had been standing in still water; but her thoughts had been given a rough jerk inward, her outward vision fell no deeper than the polished surface, while her mind's eye saw all at once the dusty veranda boards of Wallandoon. She stood very still, and in her ears the music died away, and through three months of travel and great changes she heard again the night-horse champing in the yard, and the crickets chirping further afield. And as she stood, her head bowed by this sudden memory, footsteps approached, and she looked up, expecting to see Herbert. But it was not Herbert; it was a young man of more visible distinction than Herbert Luttrell. It is difficult to look better dressed than another in our evening mode; but this young man overcame the difficulty. He stood erect; he was well built; his clothes fitted beautifully; he was himself nice looking, and fair-haired, and boyish; and, even more than his clothes, one admired his smile, which was frank and delightful. But the smile he gave Christina was followed by a blush, for she had held out her hand to him, and asked him how he was.

"I'm all right, thanks. But—this is the most extraordinary thing! Been over long?"

He had dropped her hand.

"About a fortnight," said Christina.

"But what a pity to come over so late in the season! It's about done, you know."

"Yes. I thought there was a good deal going on still."

"There's Henley, to be sure."

"I think I'm going to Henley."

"Going to the Eton and Harrow?"

"I am not quite sure. That was your match, wasn't it?"

The young man blushed afresh.

"Fancy your remembering! Unfortunately it wasn't my match, though; my day out was against Winchester."

"Oh, yes," said Tiny, less knowingly.

"And how are you, Miss Luttrell?"

This had been forgotten, Tiny reported well of herself. Her friend hesitated; there was some nervousness in his manner, but his good eyes never fell from her face, and presently he exclaimed, as though the idea had just struck him:

"I say, mayn't I have this dance, Miss Luttrell—what's left of it?"

"Thanks, I'm afraid I'm engaged for it."

"Then mayn't I find your partner for you?"

Now this second request, or his anxious way of making it, was an elaborate revelation to Christina, and wrote itself in her brain. "Do you remember Herbert?" she, however, simply replied. "He is the culprit."

"Your brother? Certainly I remember him. I saw him a few minutes ago, and made sure I had seen him somewhere before; but he looks older. I don't fancy he's dancing. He's somewhere or other with somebody in red."

"So I hear."

"Then mayn't I have a turn with you before it stops?"

She hesitated as long as he had hesitated before first asking her; there was not time to hesitate longer. Then she took his arm, and they passed through a narrow avenue of ferns and flowers, round a corner, up some steps, and so into the ball room.

The waltz was indeed half over, but the second half of it Christina and her fortuitous partner danced together, without a rest, and also without a word. He led her a more enterprising measure than those previous partners who had questioned her concerning Australia. The name of Australia had not crossed this one's lips. As Tiny whirled and glided on his arm she saw a good many eyes upon her: they made her dance her best; and her best was the best in the room, though her partner was uncommonly good, and they had danced together before. Among the eyes were Ruth's, and they were beaming; the others were mostly inquisitive, and as strange to Christina as she evidently was to them; but once a turn brought her face to face with Herbert, on his way from the conservatory, and alone. He was a lanky, brown-faced, hook-nosed boy, with wiry limbs and an aggressive eye, and he followed his sister round the room with a stare of which she was uncomfortably conscious. He had looked for her too late, when forced to relinquish the girl in red to her proper partner, who still seemed put out. Christina was put out also, by her brother's look, but she did not show it.

"You are staying in town?" her partner said after the dance as they sat together in the conservatory, but not in the old corner.

"Yes, with my sister, Mrs. Holland; you never met her, I think. We are in town till August."

"Where do you go then?"

"To the country for a month. My sister and her husband have taken a country rectory for the whole of August. They had it last year, and liked the place so much that they have taken it again; it is a little village called Essingham."

"Essingham!" cried Christina's partner.

"Yes; do you know it?"

"I know of it," answered the young man. "I suppose you will go on the Continent after that?" he added quickly.

"Well, hardly; my brother-in-law has so little time; but he expects to have to go to Lisbon on business at the end of October, and he has promised to take us with him."

"To Lisbon at the end of October," repeated Tiny's friend reflectively. "Get him to take you to Cintra. They say it's well worth seeing."

Yet another dance was beginning. Christina was interested in the movements of a young man in spectacles, who was plainly in search of somebody. "He's hunting for me," she whispered to her companion, who was saying:

"Portugal's rather the knuckle end of Europe, don't you think? But I've heard Cintra well spoken of. I should go there if I were you."

"We intend to. Do you mind pulling that young man's coat tails? He has forgotten my face."

"Yes, I do mind," said Tiny's partner with unexpected earnestness. "I may meet you again, but I should like to take this opportunity of explaining——"

Tiny Luttrell was smiling in his face.

"I hate explanations!" she cried. "They are an insult to one's imagination, and I much prefer to accept things without them." There was a gleam in her smile, but as she spoke she flashed it upon the spectacles of her blind pursuer, who was squaring his arm to her in an instant.

And that was the last she saw of the only partner for whom she had a good word afterward, and he had come to her by accident. But it was by no means the last she heard of him. The next was from Herbert, as they drove home together in one hansom, while Ruth and her husband followed in another. The morning air blew fresh upon their faces; the rising sun struck sparks from the harness; the leaves in the park were greener than any in Australia, and the dew on the grass through the railings was as a silver shower new-fallen. But the most delicious taste of London that had yet been given her was poisoned for Christina by her brother Herbert.

"To have my claim jumped by that joker!" said he through his nose.

"But you had left it empty," said Tiny mildly. "I was all alone."

"It isn't so much that," her brother said, shifting the ground he had taken in preliminary charges; "it's your dancing with that brute Manister!"

"My dear old Herbs," said Miss Luttrell with provoking coolness, "Lord Manister asked me to dance with him, and I didn't see why I should refuse. I certainly didn't see why I should consult you, Herbs."

"By ghost," cried Herbert, "if it comes to that, he once asked you to marry him!"

"Now you are a treat," said the girl, before the blood came.

"And then bolted! I should be ashamed of myself for dancing with him if I were you. He said I was a larrikin, too. I'd like to fill his eye for him!"

"He'll never say a truer thing!" Christina cried out; but her voice broke over the words, and the early sun cut diamonds on her lashes.

Now this was Herbert: he was rough, but not cowardly. His nose had become hooked in his teens from a stand-up fight with a full-grown man. There is not the least doubt that in such a combat with Lord Manister that nobleman, though otherwise a finer athlete, would have suffered extremely. But it was not in Herbert to hit any woman in cold blood with his tongue. Having done this in his heat to Christina, his mate, he was man enough to be sorry and ashamed, and to slip her hands into his.

"I'm an awful beast," he stammered out. "I didn't mean anything at all—except that I'd like to fill up Manister's eye! I can't go back on that when—when he called me a larrikin!"

CHAPTER IV.
RUTH AND CHRISTINA.

Here is the difference between Ruth and Christina, who were considered so much alike.

Of the two, Ruth was the one to fall in love with at sight—of which Erskine Holland supplies the proof. She was less diminutive than her sister; she had a finer figure, a warmer color, and indeed, despite the destructive Australian sun, a very beautiful complexion. In the early days at Wallandoon she had given herself a better chance in this respect than Christina had done, not from vanity at all, but rather owing to certain differences in their ideas of pleasure, into which it is needless to enter. The result was her complexion; and this was not her only beauty, for she had good brown eyes that suited her coloring as autumn leaves befit an autumn sunset. These eyes are never unkind, but Ruth's were sweet-tempered to a fault. So the glance of one scanning both girls for the first time rested naturally upon Ruth, but on all subsequent occasions it flew straight to Christina, because there was an end to Ruth; but there was no coming to an end of Tiny, about whom there was ever some fresh thing to charm or disappoint one.

Thus, but for the businesslike dispatch of Erskine Holland, it might have been Ruth's fate to break in Christina's admirers until Christina fancied one of them enough to marry him. For Ruth's was perhaps the more unselfish character of the two, as it was certainly the simpler one, in spite of a peculiar secretive strain in her from which Tiny was free. Tiny, on the other hand, was much more sensitive; but to perceive this was to understand her better than she understood herself. For she did not know her own weaknesses as the self-examining know theirs, and hardly anybody suspected her of this one until her arrival in England—when Erskine Holland came to treat her as a sister, and to understand her more or less.

In Australia he had seen very little of her, though enough to regard her at the time as an arrant little heartless flirt, for whom sighed silly swains innumerable. That she was, indeed, a flirt there was still no denying; but as his knowledge of her ripened, Holland was glad to unharness the opprobrious epithets with which Ruth's sister had first driven herself into his mind. He discovered good points in Christina, and among them a humor which he had never detected out in Australia. Probably his own sense of it had lost its edge out there, for love-making blunts nothing sooner; while Ruth, for her part, was naturally wanting in humor. Holland had never been blind to this defect in his wife, but he seemed resigned to it; one can conceive it to be a merit in the wife of an amusing man.

Some people called Erskine amusing—it is not hard to win this label from some people—but at any rate he was never likely to find it difficult to amuse Ruth. Now no companion in this world is more charming for all time than the person who is content to do the laughing. As a novelty, however, Christina had her own distinctive attraction for Erskine Holland. And they got on so well together that presently he saw more in Tiny than her humor, which others had seen before him; he saw that her heart was softer than she thought; but he divined that something had happened to harden it.

"She has been falling in love," he said to Ruth—"and something has happened."

"What makes you think so? She has told me nothing about it," Ruth said.

"Ah, she is sensitive. I can see that, too. It's her bitterness, however, that makes me think something has turned out badly."

"She is sadly cynical," remarked Ruth.

"Cynically sad, I rather think," her husband said. "I don't fancy she's languishing now; I should say she has got over the thing, whatever it has been—and is rather disappointed with herself for getting over it so easily. She has hinted at nothing, but she has a trick of generalizing; and she affects to think that one person doesn't fret for another longer than a week in real life. I don't say her cynicism is so much affectation; something or other has left a bad taste in her mouth; but I should like to bet that it wasn't an affair of the most serious sort."

"Her affairs never were very serious, Erskine."

"So I gathered from what I saw of her before we were married. It's a pity," said Erskine musingly. "I'd like to see her married, but I'd love to see her wooed! That's where the sport would come in. There would be no knowing where the fellow had her. He might hook her by luck, but he'd have to play her like fun before he landed her! There'd be a strong sporting interest in the whole thing, and that's what one likes."

"It's a pity I didn't know what you liked," Ruth said, with a smile; "and a wonder that you liked me, and not Tiny!"

"My darling," laughed her husband, "that sort of sport's for the young fellows. I'm past it. I merely meant that I should like to see the sport. No, Tiny's charming in her way, but God forbid that it should be your way too!"

Now Ruth was such a fond little wife that at this speech she became too much gratified on her own account to care to discuss her sister any further. But in dismissing the subject of Tiny she took occasion to impress one fact upon Erskine:

"You may be right, dear, and something may have happened since I left home; but I can only tell you that Tiny hasn't breathed a single word about it to me."

And this is an early sample of the disingenuous streak that was in the very grain of Ruth. Christina, indeed, had told her nothing, but Ruth knew nearly all that there was to know of the affair whose traces were plain to her husband's insight. Beyond the fact that the name of Tiny Luttrell had been coupled in Melbourne with that of Lord Manister, and the *on dit* that Lord Manister had treated her rather badly, there was, indeed, very little to be known. But Ruth knew at least as much as her mother, who had written to her on the subject the more freely and frequently because her younger daughter flatly refused the poor lady her confidence. There was no harm in Ruth's not showing those letters to her husband. There was no harm in her keeping her sister's private affairs from her husband's knowledge. There was the reverse of harm in both reservations, as Erskine would have been the first to allow. Ruth had her reasons for making them; and if her reasons embodied a deep design, there was no harm in that either, for surely it is permissible to plot and scheme for the happiness of another. I can see no harm in her conduct from any point of view. But it was certainly disingenuous, and it entailed an insincere attitude toward two people, which in itself was not admirable. And those two were her nearest. However amiable her plans might be, they made it impossible for Ruth to be perfectly sincere with her husband on one subject, which was bad enough. But with Christina it was still more impossible to be at all candid; and this happened to be worse, for reasons which will be recognized later. In the first place, Tiny immediately discovered Ruth's insincerity, and even her plans. Tiny was a difficult person to deceive. She detected the insincerity in a single conversation with Ruth on the afternoon following Lady Almeric's ball, and before she went to bed she was as much in possession of the plans as if Ruth had told her them.

The conversation took place in Erskine's study, where the sisters had foregathered for a lazy afternoon.

"Oh, by the way," said Ruth, apropos of the ball, "it was a coincidence your dancing with Lord Manister."

"Why a coincidence?" asked Christina. She glanced rather sharply at Ruth as she put the question.

"Well, it is just possible that we shall see something of him in the country. That's all," said Ruth, as she bent over the novel of which she was cutting the pages.

Christina also had a book in her lap, but she had not opened it; she was trying to read Ruth's averted face.

"I thought perhaps you meant because we saw something of him in Melbourne," she said presently. "I suppose you know that we did see something of him? He even honored us once or twice."

"So you told me in your letters."

The paper knife was still at work.

"What makes it likely that we shall see him in the country?"

"Well, Mundham Hall is quite close to Essingham, you know."

"Mundham Hall! Whose place is that?"

"Lord Dromard's," replied Ruth, still intent upon her work.

"Surely not!" exclaimed Christina. "Lord Manister once told me the name of their place, and I am convinced it wasn't that."

"They have several places. But until quite lately they have lived mostly at the other side of the county, at Wreford Abbey."

"That was the name."

"But they have sold that place," said Ruth, "and last autumn Lord Dromard bought Mundham; it was empty when we were at Essingham last year."

For some moments there was silence, broken only by the leisurely swish of Ruth's paper knife. Then Christina said, "That accounts for it," thinking aloud.

"For what?" asked Ruth rather nervously.

"Lord Manister told me he knew of Essingham. He never mentioned Mundham. Is it so very close to your rectory?"

"The grounds are; they are very big; the hall itself is miles from the gates—almost as far as our home station was from the boundary fence."

"Surely not," Tiny said quietly.

"Well, that's a little exaggeration, of course."

"Then I wish it wasn't!" Tiny cried out. "I don't relish the idea of living under the lee of such very fine people," she said next moment, as quietly as before.

"No more do I—no more does Erskine," Ruth made haste to declare. "But we enjoyed ourselves so much there last August that we said at the time that we would take the rectory again this August. We made the people promise us the refusal. And it seemed absurd to refuse just because Lord Dromard had bought Mundham; shouldn't you have said so yourself, dear?"

"Certainly I should," answered Tiny; and for half an hour no more was said.

The afternoon was wet; there was no inducement to go out, even with the necessary energy, and the two young women, on whose pillows the sun had lain before their faces, felt anything but energetic. The afternoon was also cold to Australian blood, and a fire had been lighted in Erskine's den. His favorite armchair contained several cushions and Christina—who might as well have worn his boots—while Ruth, having cut all the leaves of her volume, curled herself up on the sofa with an obvious intention. She was good at cutting the leaves of a new book, but still better at going to sleep over them when cut. She had read even less than Christina, and it troubled her less; but this afternoon she read more. Ruth could not sleep. No more could Tiny. But Tiny had not opened her book. It was one of the good books that Erskine had lent her. She was extremely interested in it; but just at present her own affairs interested her more. Lying back in the big chair, with the wet gray light behind her, and that of the fire playing fitfully over her face, Christina committed what was as yet an unusual weakness for her, by giving way voluntarily to her thoughts. She was in the habit of thinking as little as possible, because so many of her thoughts were depressing company, and beyond all things she disliked being depressed. This afternoon she was less depressed than indignant. The firelight showed her forehead strung with furrows. From time to time she turned her eyes to the sofa, as if to make sure that Ruth was still awake, and as often as they rested there they gleamed. At last she spoke Ruth's name.

"Well?" said Ruth. "I thought you were asleep; you have never stirred."

"I'm not sleepy, thanks; and, if you don't mind, I should like to speak to you before you drop off yourself."

Ruth closed her novel.

"What is it, dear? I'm listening."

"When you wrote and invited me over you mentioned Essingham as one of the attractions. Now why couldn't you tell me the Dromards would be our neighbors there?"

Ruth raised her eyes from the younger girl's face to the rain-spattered window. Tiny's tone was cold, but not so cold as Tiny's searching glance. This made Ruth uncomfortable. It did not incapacitate her, however.

"The Dromards!" she exclaimed rather well. "Had they taken the place then?"

"You say they bought it before Christmas; it was after Christmas that you first wrote and expressly invited me."

"Was it? Well, my dear, I suppose I never thought of them; that's all. They aren't the only nice people thereabouts."

"I'm afraid you are not quite frank with me," the young girl said; and her own frankness was a little painful.

"Tiny, dear, what a thing to say! What does it mean?"

Ruth employed for these words the injured tone.

"It means that you know as well as I do, Ruth, that it isn't pleasant for me to meet Lord Manister."

"Was there something between you in Melbourne?" asked Ruth. "I must say that nobody would have thought so from seeing you together last night. And—and how was I to think so, when you have never told me anything about it?"

Christina laughed bitterly.

"When you have made a fool of yourself you don't go out of your way to talk about it, even to your own people. It is kind of you to pretend to know nothing about it—I am sure you mean it kindly; but I'm still surer that you have been told all there was to tell concerning Lord Manister and me. I don't mean by Herbert. He's close. But the mother must have written and told you something; it was only natural that she should do so."

"She did tell me a little. Herbert has told me nothing. I tried to pump him,—I think you can't wonder at that,—but he refused to speak a word on the subject. He says he hates it."

"He hates Lord Manister," said Christina, smiling. "It came round to him once that Lord Manister had called him a larrikin, and he has never forgiven him. But he has been less of a larrikin ever since. And, of course, that wasn't why he was so angry with me for dancing with Lord Manister last night; he was dreadfully angry with me as we drove home; but he is a very good boy to me, and there was something in what he said."

"What made you dance with him?" Ruth said curiously.

"I was alone. I hadn't a partner. He asked me rather prettily—he always had pretty manners. You wouldn't have had me show him I cared, by snubbing him, would you?"

"No," said Ruth thoughtfully; and suddenly she slipped from the sofa, and was kneeling on the hearthrug, with her brown eyes softly searching

Christina's face and her lips whispering, "Do you care, Tiny? *Do* you care, Tiny, dear?"

Tiny snapped her fingers as she pushed back her chair.

"Not that much for anybody—much less for Lord Manister, and least of all for myself! Now don't you be too good to me, Ruth; if you are you'll only make me feel ungrateful, and I shall run away, because I'm not going to tell you another word about what's over and done with. I can't! I have got over the whole thing, but it has been a sickener. It makes me sick to think about it. I don't want ever to speak of it again."

"I understand," said Ruth; but there was disappointment in her look and tone, and she added, "I should like to have heard the truth, though; and no one can tell it me but you."

"I thank Heaven for that!" cried Christina piously. "The version out there was that he proposed to me and I accepted him, and then he bolted without even saying good-by. It's true that he didn't say good-by; the rest is not true. But you must just make it do."

Her face was scarlet with the shame of it all; but there was no sign of weakness in the curling lips. She spoke bitterly, but not at all sadly, and her next words were still more suggestive of a wound to the vanity rather than to the heart.

"Does Erskine know?"

"Not a word."

"Honestly?"

"Quite honestly; at least I have never mentioned it to him, and I don't think anybody else has, or he would have mentioned it to me."

"Oh, Herbert wouldn't say anything. Herbert's very close. But—don't you two tell each other everything, Ruth?"

The young girl looked incredulous; the married woman smiled.

"Hardly everything, you know! Erskine has lots of relations himself, for instance, and I'm sure he wouldn't care to tell me the ins and outs of their private affairs, even if I cared to know them. It's just the same about you and your affairs, don't you see."

"Except that he knows me so well," Christina reflected aloud, with her eyes upon the fire. "If I had a husband," she added impulsively, "I should like to tell him every mortal thing, whether I wanted to or not! And I should like not to want to, but to be made. But that's because I should like above all things to be bossed!"

"You would take some bossing," suggested Ruth.

"That's the worst of it," said Christina, with a little sigh, and then a laugh, as she snatched her eyes from the fire. "But I can't tell you how glad I am you haven't told Erskine. Never tell him, Ruth, for you don't know how I covet his good opinion. I like him, you know, dear, and I rather think he likes me—so far."

"Indeed he does," cried Ruth warmly; and a good point in her character stood out through the genuine words. "Nothing ever made me happier than to see you become such friends."

"He laughs at me a good deal," Tiny remarked doubtfully.

"That's because you amuse him a good deal. I can't get him to laugh at me, my dear."

"He would laugh," said Christina, with her eyes on the fire again, "if you told him I had aspired to Lord Manister!"

"But I'm not going to tell him anything at all about it." Ruth paused. "And after all, the Dromards won't take any notice of us in the country." She paused again. "And we won't speak of this any more, Tiny, if you don't like."

The shame had come back to Christina's face as she bent it toward the fire. Twice she had made no answer to what was kindly meant and even kindlier said. But now she turned and kissed Ruth, saying, "Thank you, dear. I am afraid I don't like. But you have been awfully good and sweet about it—as I shan't forget." And the fire lit their faces as they met, but the tear that had got upon Tiny's cheek was not her own.

Ruth, you see, could be tender and sympathetic and genuine enough. But she could not be sensible and let well alone.

She did that night a very foolish thing: she brought up the subject again. Tempted she certainly was. Never since her arrival in England had Tiny seemed so near to her or she to Tiny as in the hours immediately following the chat between them in Erskine's study. But Christina stood further from Ruth than Ruth imagined; she had not advanced, but retreated, before the glow of Ruth's sympathy. This was after the event, when some hours separated Christina from those emotional moments to which she had not contributed her share of the emotion, leaving the scene upon her mind in just perspective. She still could value Ruth's sweetness at the end of their talk, but her own suspicions, aroused at the outset, to be immediately killed by a little kindness, had come to life again, and were calling for an equal appreciation. The extent of Tiny's suspicions was very full, and the suspicions themselves were uncommonly shrewd and convincing. They made it a little hard to return Ruth's smiles during the evening, and to kiss her when saying good-night, though Tiny did these things duly. She went upstairs before her time, however, and not at all in the mood to be bothered any further about Lord Manister. Yet she behaved very patiently when Ruth came presently to her room and thus bothered her, being suddenly tempted beyond her strength. For Christina was discovered standing fully dressed under the gas-bracket, and frowning at a certain photograph on an orange-colored mount, which she turned face downward as Ruth entered. Whereupon Ruth, discerning the sign manual of a Melbourne photographer, could not help saying slyly, "Who is it, Tiny?"

"A friend of mine," Tiny said, also slyly, but keeping the photograph itself turned provokingly to the floor.

"In Australia?"

"Er—it was taken out there."

"It's Lord Manister!"

"Perhaps it is—perhaps it isn't."

"Tiny," said Ruth with pathos, "you might show me!"

But Tiny drummed vexatiously on the wrong side of the mount; and here Ruth surely should have let the matter drop, instead of which:

"You are very horrid," she said, "but I must just tell you something. I have heard things from Lady Almeric, who is very intimate with Lady Dromard, and I don't believe *he* is so much to blame as you think him. I have heard it spoken about in society. But don't look frightened. Your name has never been mentioned. I don't think it has ever come out. Indeed, I know it hasn't, for *I*, actually, have been asked the name of the girl Lord Manister was fond of in Melbourne—by Lady Almeric!"

"And what did you say?"

"What do you suppose? I glory in that fib—I am honestly proud of it. But, dear, the point is, not that Lord Manister has never mentioned your name, but that he can bear neither name nor sight of the girl he is expected to marry! Lady Almeric told me when—I couldn't help her."

"He is a nice young man, I must say!" remarked Christina grimly. "My fellow-victim has a title, no doubt?"

"Well, it's Miss Garth, and her father's Lord Acklam, so she's the honorable," said Ruth gravely. (Tiny smiled at her gravity.) "But I've seen her, and—he can't like her! And oh! Tiny dear, they all say he left his heart in Australia, but his mother sent for him because she heard something—but not your name, dear—and he came. They say he is devoted to his mother; but this has come between them, and she's sorry she interfered, because after all he won't marry poor Miss Garth. I had it direct from Lady Almeric when she tried to get that out of me. But I lied like a trooper!" exclaimed poor Ruth.

"I'm grateful to you for that," Christina said, not ungraciously—"but I must really be going to bed."

With a last wistful glance at the orange-colored cardboard, Ruth took the hint. Christina turned away in time to avoid an embrace without showing her repugnance, because she had still some regard for Ruth's good heart. But she had never experienced a more grateful riddance, and the look that followed Ruth to the threshold would have kept her company for some time had she turned there and caught one glimpse of it.

"Now I understand!" said Christina to the closed door. "I suppose I ought to love you for it, Ruth; but I don't—no, I don't!"

She turned the photograph face upward, and stared thoughtfully at it for some minutes longer; then she put it away.

CHAPTER V.
ESSINGHAM RECTORY.

Essingham Rectory, which the Erskine Hollands had taken for the month of August, was a little old building with some picturesque points to console one for the tameness of the view from its windows. The surrounding country was perfectly flat but for Gallow Hill, and not at all green but for the glebe and the riverside meadows, while the only trees of any account were the rectory elms and those in the Mundham grounds. It is true that on Gallow Hill three wind-crippled beeches brandished their deformities against the sky, as they may do still; but the country around Essingham is no country for trees. It is the country for warrens and rabbits and roads without hedges. So it struck Christina as more like the back-blocks than anything she had hoped to see in England, and pleased her more than anything she had seen. She showed her pleasure before they arrived at Essingham. She forgot to disparage the old country during the long drive from the county town; and that was notable. She had actually no stone to cast at the elaborate and impressive gates of Mundham Hall; apparently she was herself impressed. But opposite the gates they turned to the left, into a narrow road with hedges, from which you can see the rectory, and as Herbert put it afterward:

"That's what knocked our Tiny!"

For the girl's first glimpse of the old house was over the hedge and far away above a brilliant sash of meadow green. The cream-colored walls were aglow in the low late sunshine, what was to be seen of them, for they were half hidden by a creeper almost as old as themselves. The red-tiled, weather-beaten roof was dark with age. Even at a distance one smelt rats in the wainscot within the stuccoed walls. Around the house, and towering above the tiles, the elms stood as still against the evening sky as the square church tower but a little way to the right. To the right of that, but farther away, rose Gallow Hill. Thereabouts the sun was sinking, but the clock on the near side of the church tower had gilt hands, which marked the hour when Christina stood up in the fly and astonished her friends with her frank delight. It was a point against this young lady, on subsequent occasions when she did not forget to decry the old country, that at ten minutes past seven on the evening of the 1st of August she had given way to enthusiasm over a scene that was purely English and very ordinary in itself.

Not that her immediate appreciation of the place became modified on a closer acquaintance with it. At the end of the first clear day at Essingham she informed the others that thus far she had not enjoyed herself so much since leaving Australia. Of course she had enjoyed herself in London. That did not count. London only compared itself with Melbourne, Christina did not care how favorably; but Essingham was for comparison with the place that was dearer to her than any other in the world. You will understand why all her appreciations were directly comparative. This is natural in the very young, and fortunately Tiny Luttrell was still very young in some respects. Blessed with observant eyes, and having at this time an irritable memory to keep her prejudices at attention, her mind soon became the scene of many curious and specific contests between England and Australia. In the match between Wallandoon and Essingham the latter made a better fight than you would think against so strong an opponent. The rectory was homely and convenient in its old age, and Christina was greatly charmed with her own room, because it was small; and if the wall-paper was modern and conventional, and not to be read from the pillow in the early morning, it was almost as pleasant to lie and watch the elm tops trembling against the sky. And if the sky was not really blue in England, the leaves in Australia were not really green, as Christina now knew. So there they were quits. But England and Essingham scored palpably in some things; the kitchen garden was one. Christina had never seen such a kitchen garden; she found it possible to spend half an hour there at any time, to her further contentment; and there were other attractions on the premises, which were just as good in their way, while their way was often better for one.

For instance, there was a lawn tennis court which satisfied the soul of Erskine, who played daily for its express refreshment. That was what brought him to Essingham. The neighboring clergy were always ready for a game. But they laughed at Erskine for being so keen; he would get up before breakfast to roll the court, which passed their understanding. Christina played also, by no means ill, and Herbert uncommonly well; but this player neither won nor lost very prettily. He was more amiable over the photography which he had taken up in partnership with Tiny; but his photographs were uncommonly bad. Yet this was another amusement in the country, where, however, Christina was most amused by the neighbors who called. These were friendly people, and they had all called on the Hollands the previous year. Half of them were clergymen, though the stranger who met them found this difficult to believe in some cases; the other half were the clergymen's wives. Very grand families apart, there is no other society round about Essingham. And what could man wish better? Even Christina found it impossible to disapprove of the well-bred, easy-going, tennis-playing, unprofessional country clergy, as acquaintances and friends. But she did find fault with the rector of Essingham as a rector, though she had never seen him, and though Ruth assured her that he was a dear old man.

"He may be a dear old man," Miss Luttrell would allow, "but he's a bad old rector! His flock don't find him such a dear old man, either. They only see him once a week, in the pulpit; and then they can't hear him!"

"Who has been telling you that, Tiny?" asked Ruth.

"You've been talking sedition in the village!" said Erskine Holland.

"Well, I've been making friends with two or three of the people, if that's what you call talking sedition," Tiny replied; "and I think your dear old rector neglects them shamefully. He does worse than that. There's some fund or other for buying coals and blankets for the poor of the parish; and there's old Mrs. Clapperton. Mrs. Clapperton's a Roman Catholic; so, if you please, she never gets her coals or blankets, and she's too proud to ask for them. That's a fact—and I tell you what, I'd like to expose your dear old man, Ruth! As for the village, if it's a specimen of your English villages, let me tell you, Erskine, that it's leagues behind the average bush township. Why, they haven't even got a state school, but only a one-horse affair run by the rector! And the schoolmaster's the most ignorant man in the village. I wonder you don't copy us, and go in for state schools!"

"'Copy us, and go in for state schools,'" echoed Ruth with gentle mirth, as she sometimes would echo Tiny's remarks, and with a smile that traveled from Tiny to Erskine. But Erskine did not return the smile. His eyes rested shrewdly upon Christina, and Ruth feared from their expression that he thought the girl an utter fool; but she was wrong.

Christina was not, if you like, an intellectual girl, but she was by no means a fool. Neither was her brother-in-law, who perceived this. Her comments on the books he lent her were sufficiently intelligent, and she pleased him in other ways too. He was glad, for instance, to see her interesting herself in the local peasants; she was particularly glad that she did not give this interest its head, though as a matter of fact it never pulled. Christina was not the girl for interests that gallop and have not legs. Not the least of her attractions, in the eyes of a male relative of middle age, was a certain solid sanity that showed through every crevice of her wayward nature. It was sanity of the cynical sort, which men appreciate most. And it was least apparent in her own actions, which is the weak point of the cynically sane.

"At all events, Tiny, you can't find the country a tight fit, like London," said Erskine once, during the first few days. "Come, now!"

"No," replied Tiny thoughtfully, "I must own it doesn't fit so tight. But it tickles! You mayn't go here and you mayn't go there; in Australia you may go anywhere you darn please. Excuse me, Erskine, but I feel this a good deal. Only this morning Ruth and I were blocked by a notice board just outside the wicket at the far end of the churchyard; we were thinking of going up Gallow Hill, but we had to turn back, as trespassers would be prosecuted. There's no trespassing where I come from. And Ruth says the board wasn't there last year."

"Ah, the Dromards weren't there last year! They've stuck it up. You should pitch into your friend Lord Manister. It's rather vexatious of them, I grant you; they can't want to have tea on Gallow Hill; and it's a pity, because there's a fine view of the Hall from the top."

"Indeed? Ruth never told me that," remarked Christina curiously. "Have they arrived yet?" she added in apparent idleness.

"Last night, I hear—if you mean the Dromards. And a rumor has arrived with them."

Now Christina was careful not to inquire what the rumor was; but Erskine told her; and, oddly enough, what he had heard and now repeated was to come true immediately.

The great family at Mundham were about to entertain the county. That was the whisper, which was presently to be spoken aloud as a pure fact. It ran over the land with "At last!" hissing at its heels, and a still more sinister whisper chased the pair of them; for the Dromards might have entertained the county months before; a house-warming had been expected of them in the winter, but they had chosen to warm Mundham with their own friends from a distance; and since then the general election had become a moral certainty for the following spring, and—the point was—Viscount Manister had declared his willingness to stand for the division. The corollary was irresistible, but so, it appears, was Countess Dromard's invitation, which few are believed to have declined—for those that did so made it known. Some disgust, however, was expressed at the kind of entertainment, which, after all, was to be nothing more than a garden party. But nearly all who were bidden accepted. The notice, too, was shorter than other people would have presumed to give; but other people were not the Dromards. The countess' invitation conveyed to a hundred country homes a joy that was none the less keen for a certain shame or shyness in showing any sort of satisfaction in so small a matter. Nevertheless, though not adorned by a coronet, as it might have been, nor in any way a striking trophy, the card obtained a telling position over many a rectory chimney-piece, where in some instances it remained, accidentally, for months. In justice to the residents, however, it must be owned that not one of them read it with a more poignant delight, nor adjusted it in the mirror with a nicer care and a finer show of carelessness, nor gazed at it oftener while ostensibly looking at the clock, than did Mrs. Erskine Holland during the next ten days.

But when it came she acted cleverly. There was occasion for all her cleverness, because in her case the invitation was a complete surprise; she had not dared to expect one; and you may imagine her peculiar satisfaction at receiving an invitation that embraced her "party." Yet she was able to toss the card across the breakfast table to Erskine, merely remarking, "Should we go?" And when Tiny at once stated that for her part she was not keen, Ruth gave her a sympathetic look, as much as to say, "No more am I, my dear," which might have deceived a less discerning person. But Tiny saw that her sister was holding her breath until Erskine spoke his mind.

"Have we any other engagement?" said he directly. "If not, it would hardly do to stick here playing tennis within sight of their lodge. I'm no more keen than you are, Tiny, but that would look uncommon poor. It was very kind of them to think of asking us; I'm afraid we must go; but I am sure you will find it amusing."

"Thanks," replied Christina, to whom this assurance was addressed, "but you needn't send me there to be amused; you see, I have plenty to amuse me here," she added, with a smile that had been slow to come. "I'll go, of course, and with pleasure; but there would be more pleasure in some hard sets with you, Erskine, or in taking your photograph."

"Ah, you don't know what you'd miss, Tiny! I can promise you some sport, if you keep your eyes and ears open. Then you knew Lord Manister in Melbourne. In any case, you oughtn't to go back there without a glimpse of some of our fine folks at home, when you can get it."

"Oh, I'll go; but not for the sport of seeing your clergy and gentry on their knees to your fine folks, nor yet to be amused. As for Lord Manister, he was well enough in Melbourne; he didn't give himself airs, and there he was wise. But on his native heath! One would be sorry to set foot on the same soil. It must be sacred."

"Come, I say, I don't think you'll find the parsons on their knees. We think a lot of a lord, if you like; but we try to forget that when we're talking to him. We do our best to treat him as though he were merely a gentleman, you know," said Erskine, smiling, but giving, as he felt, an informing hint.

"Ah, you try!" said Christina. "You do your best!"

"Our best may be very bad," laughed Erskine; "if so, you must show us how to better it, Tiny."

"I should get Tiny to teach you how to treat a lord, dear," said Ruth, who saw nothing to laugh at, and seemed likely to lend her husband a severer support than the occasion needed.

"Say Lord Manister!" suggested Erskine. "Will you show me on him?"

"I may if you're good—you wait and see," said Tiny lightly. And lightly the matter was allowed to drop. For Herbert, as usual, was late for breakfast, which was for once a very good thing; and as for Ruth, it was merely her misfortune to have a near sight for the line dividing chaff from earnest, but now she saw it, and on which side of it the others were, for she had joined them and was laughing herself.

But Herbert would not have laughed at all; indeed, he had not a smile for the subject when he did come down and Ruth gave him his breakfast alone. It seemed well that Christina was not in the room. Her brother took the opportunity of saying what he thought of Manister, and what Manister had once called him behind his back, and what he would have done to Manister's eye had half as much been said to his face. His personal decision about the garden party was merely contemptuous. He was not going. Nor did he go when the time came. Meanwhile, however, something happened to modify for the moment his opinion of the young viscount whom it was Herbert's meager satisfaction to abuse roundly whenever his noble name was spoken.

Having been provided with two rooms at the rectory, in one of which he was expected to read diligently every morning, Herbert entered that room only when his pipe needed filling. He kept his tobacco there, and also, to be sure, his books; but these he never opened. He read nothing, save chance items in an occasional sporting paper; he simply smoked and pottered, leaving the smell of his pipe in the least desirable places. When he took photographs with Tiny, that was pottering too, for neither of them knew much about it, and Herbert was too indolent to take either pains or care in a pursuit which essentially demands both. He had rather a good eye for a subject; he could arrange a picture with some judgment. That interested him, but the subsequent processes did not, and these invariably spoilt the plate. All his actions, however, suggested an underlying theory that what is worth doing is not necessarily worth doing well. This applied even to his games, about which Herbert was really keen; he played lawn tennis carelessly, though with a verve and energy somewhat surprising in the loafing, smoking idler of the morning. He had been fond of cricket, too, in Australia; it was a disappointment to him that no cricket was to be had at Essingham. He looked forward to Cambridge for the athletic advantages. He had no intention of reading there; so what, he wanted to know, was the good of his reading here? Certainly Herbert had entered at an accommodating college, which would receive young men quite free from previous knowledge; but he might have been reading for his little-go all this time; and he never read a word.

But one morning he loitered afield, and came back enthusiastic about a place for a photograph; the next, Tiny and the implements were dragged to the spot; and really it was not bad. It was a scene on the little river just below Mundham bridge. The thick white rails of the bridge standing out against a clump of trees in the park beyond, the single arch with the dark water underneath and some sunlit ripples twinkling at the further side, seemed to call aloud for a camera; and Herbert might have used his to some purpose, for a change, had he not forgotten to fill his slides with plates before leaving home. This discovery was not made until the bridge was in focus, and it put young Luttrell in the plight of a rifleman who has sighted the bull's-eye with an empty barrel. It was a question of returning to the rectory to load the slides or of giving up the photograph altogether. On another occasion, having forgotten the lens, Herbert had packed up the camera and gone back in disgust. But that happened nearer home. To-day he had carried the camera a good mile. Two journeys with something to show for them were preferable to one with a tired arm for the only result. Within a minute after the slides were found empty Christina was alone in the meadow below the bridge; Herbert had found it impossible to give up the photograph altogether.

The girl had not lost patience, for she was herself partly to blame. There were, however, still better reasons for her resignation. She happened to have the second volume of "The Newcomes" in her jacket pocket, and the little river seemed to ripple her an invitation from the bridge to make herself comfortable with her book in its shade. There was no great need for shade, but the idea seemed sensible. With her hand on the book in her pocket, and her eyes hovering about the bridge for the coolest corner, she felt perhaps a little ashamed as she thought of Herbert making a cool day hot by running back alone for what they had both forgotten. It was hardly this feeling, however, that kept her standing where she was.

She had known no finer day in England. The light was strong and limpid, the shadows abrupt and deep. The sky was not cloudless, but the clouds were thin and clean. There was a refreshing amount of wind; the tree tops beyond the bridge swayed a little against the sky; the focusing cloth flapped between the tripod legs, and for some minutes the girl stood absently imbibing all this, without a thought in her head.

Presently she found herself wondering whether there was enough movement in the trees to mar a photograph; later she tucked her head under the cloth to see. As she examined the inverted picture on the ground glass, she held the cloth loosely over her head and round her neck. But suddenly she twitched it tighter. For first the sound of wheels had come to her ears. Then a dogcart had been pulled up on the bridge. And now on the focusing screen a figure was advancing upside down, like a fly on the ceiling, and doubling its size with each stride, until there occurred a momentary eclipse of the inverted landscape by Lord Manister, who had stalked in broad daylight to our Tiny's side.

CHAPTER VI.
A MATTER OF ANCIENT HISTORY.

The focusing cloth clung to her head like a cowl as she raised it and bowed. There must have been nervousness on both sides, for the moment, but it did not prevent Lord Manister from taking off his hat with a sweep and swiftness that amounted almost to a flourish, nor Christina from noticing this and his clothes. He was so admirably attired in summer gray that she took pleasure in reflecting that she was herself unusually shabby, her idea being that contact with the incorrect was rather good for him. Correctness of any kind, it is to be feared, was ridiculously wrong in her eyes. Otherwise she might have been different herself.

"I knew it was you!" Lord Manister declared, having shaken her hand.

"How could you know?" said Christina, smiling. "You must be very clever."

"I wish I was. No; I met your brother running like anything with some wooden things under his arm. He wouldn't see me, but I saw him. I was going to pull up, but he wouldn't see me."

Miss Luttrell explained that her brother had gone back for plates, which they had both very stupidly forgotten; she added that she was sure he could not have recognized Lord Manister.

"Plates!" said this nobleman. "Ah, they're important, I know."

"Well, they're your cartridges; you can't shoot anything without them."

Lord Manister gave a louder laugh than the remark merited; then he studied his boots among the daisies. Christina smiled as she watched him, until he looked up briskly, and nearly caught her.

"I say, Miss Luttrell, I should like immensely to be on in this scene, if you would let me! I mean to say I should like to see the thing taken. Perhaps you could do with the trap and my mare on the bridge; she's something special, I assure you. And I have been thinking—if you think so too—that my man might go back for your brother and give him a lift. It must be monstrous hot walking. It's a monstrous hot day, you know."

This was not only an exaggeration, but a puff of smoke revealing hidden fires within the young man's head. Christina fanned the fire until it tinged his cheek by willfully hesitating before giving him a gracious answer. For when she spoke it was to say, with a smile at his anxiety, "Really, you are very considerate, Lord Manister, and I am sure Herbert will be grateful." They walked to the bridge, and stood upon it the next minute, watching the dogcart swing out of sight where the road bent.

"Your brother is very likely halfway back by this time," remarked Lord Manister, who would have been very sorry to believe what he was saying. "I dare say my man will pick him up directly; if so, they'll be back in a minute."

"I hope they will," said Christina—"the light is so excellent just now," she was in a hurry to add.

"Ah, the light in Australia was better for this sort of thing."

"As a rule, yes; but it would surely be difficult to beat this morning anywhere; the great thing is, over here, that you are so free from glare."

"Then you like England?"

"Well, I must say I like this corner of England; I haven't seen much else, you know."

"Good! I am glad you like this corner; you know it's ours," said the young fellow simply. Then he paused. "How strange to meet you here, though!" he added, as if he could not help it, nor the slight stress that laid itself upon the personal pronoun.

"It should rather strike me as strange to meet you," Miss Luttrell replied pointedly; "for I am sure I told you that my sister and her husband had taken Essingham Rectory for August. You may have forgotten the occasion. It was in London."

"Dear me, no, I'm not likely to forget it. To be sure you told me—at Lady Almeric's."

"Then perhaps you remember saying that you knew *of* Essingham?"

It was not, perhaps, because this was very dryly said that Lord Manister smiled. Nor was the smile one of his best, which were charming; it was visibly the expression of his nervousness, not his mirth.

"Yes, I am sorry to say I do remember that," he confessed with an awkwardness and humility which made Christina tingle in a sudden appreciation of his position in the world. "It was very foolish of me, Miss Luttrell."

"I wonder what made you?" remarked Christina reflectively, but in a friendlier tone.

"Ah! don't wonder," he said impatiently. His eyes fell upon her for one moment, then wandered down the road, as he added strangely: "You do and say so many foolish things without a decent why or wherefore. They're the things for which you never forgive yourself! They're the things for which you never hope to be forgiven!"

The girl did not look at him, but her glance chased his down the road to the bend where the dogcart had vanished and would reappear. She, however, was the next to speak, for something had occurred to her that she very much desired to explain.

"You see, I didn't know you lived here. I had never heard of Mundham when we met in town; if I had I shouldn't have known it was yours. I never dreamt that I should meet you here. You understand, Lord Manister?"

"My dear Miss Luttrell," cried Manister earnestly, "anybody could see that!"

So Christina lost nothing by her little exhibition of anxiety to impress this point upon him; for his reply was a triumphant flourish of the opinion she desired him to hold, to show her that he had it already; and his anxiety in the matter was even more apparent than her own.

"Thank you, Lord Manister," said Christina, looking him full in the face. Then her glance dropped to his hand; and his fingers were entangled in his watch-chain; and in the knowledge that the greater awkwardness was on his side she raised her eyes confidently, and met the dogged stare of a young Briton about to make a clean breast of his misdeeds.

"Do you want to know why I didn't mention our having taken this place—that time in town?"

"That depends on whether you want to tell me."

"I must tell you. It was because I feared—I mean to say, it crossed my mind—that perhaps you mightn't care to come here if you knew."

He paused and watched her. She was looking down, with her chin half buried in the focusing cloth, which had slipped from her head and fallen round her shoulders. The coolness of her face against the black velvet exasperated him, and the more so because he felt himself flushing as he added, "I see I was a fool to fear that."

"It was certainly unnecessary, Lord Manister," said the girl calmly, and not without a note of amusement in her voice.

"So you don't mind meeting one!"

"Lord Manister, I am delighted. Why should I mind?"

"You know I behaved like a brute."

"You did, I'm afraid." He winced. "You went away without saying good-by to your friends."

"I went away without saying good-by to you."

"Among others."

"No!" he cried sharply. "You and I were more than friends."

Christina drummed the ground with one foot. Her glance passed over Lord Manister's shoulder. He knew that it waited for the dogcart at the bend of the road.

"We were more than friends," he repeated desperately.

"I don't think we ever were."

"But you thought so once!"

The girl's lip curled, but her eyes still waited in the road.

"I wonder what you yourself thought once, Lord Manister?" she said quietly. "Whatever it was, it didn't last long; but I forgive that freely. Do you know why? Why, because it was exactly the same with me."

"Do you forgive me for getting you talked about?" exclaimed Lord Manister.

"Yes—because it is the only thing I have to forgive," returned Christina after a moment's hesitation. "The rest was nonsense; and I wish you wouldn't rake it up in this dreadfully serious way."

We know what Christina might mean by nonsense. Lord Manister was not the first of her friends whom she had offended by her abuse of the word. "It was not nonsense!" he cried. "It was something either better or worse. I give you my word that I honestly meant it to be something better. But my people sent for me. What could I do?"

His voice and eyes were pitiable; but Christina showed him no pity.

"What, indeed!" she said ironically. "I myself never blamed you for going. I was quite sure that you were the passive party, though others said differently. All I have to forgive is what you made other people say; but the whole affair is a matter of ancient history—and do you think we need talk about it any more, Lord Manister?"

"It is not all I have to forgive myself," he answered bitterly, disregarding her question. "If only you would hate me, I could hate myself less; but I deserve your contempt. Yet, if you knew what has been in my heart all this time, you would pity one. You have haunted me! I have been good for nothing ever since I came back to England. My people will tell you so, when you get to know them. My mother would tell you in a minute. She has never heard your name ... but she knows there was someone ... she knows there is someone still!"

Christina had colored at last; but, as she colored, the trot of a horse came gratefully to her attentive ears.

"You must think no more about it," she whispered; and her flush deepened.

"You wipe it all out?" he cried eagerly.

"Of course I do."

Her eyes met the dogcart at the bend. Herbert was in it.

"And we start afresh?"

He thought he was to get no answer. She was gazing anxiously at Herbert as the trap approached; as it drew up on the bridge she murmured, "I think we had better let well alone," without looking at Lord Manister. "Herbert, you remember Lord Manister?" she cried aloud in the same breath.

Herbert's look was not reassuring. He was, in fact, disgusted with all present but the groom, and most of all with himself, for being where he was. Nor was he the young man to trouble to hide his feelings, and he showed them now in so black a look that Christina, who knew him, was filled with apprehension. Thanks to Lord Manister's tact, that look did not last. Manister, who had his own impression of young Luttrell's character, and had not to be shrewd to guess the other's attitude toward himself, brought his most graceful manner to bear on the situation. With Tiny Luttrell, during the bad quarter of an hour which he had deserved and now endured, his best manner had not been at his command; but it returned to him with the return of the dogcart, and in time to do him a service. He had hardly shaken hands with Herbert when he asked him as an Australian, and therefore a judge, his opinion of the mare.

The touch would have been too heavy for an older man; but Herbert was barely twenty, and it flattered him to the marrow. Christina was relieved to hear his knowing but laudatory comments on the mare's points. She knew that, despite her brother's aggressive independence, he was susceptible enough to marked civility. This, indeed, he never expected, and he was ever ready to return, with interest, some fancied slight; but Christina had never known him rude to anyone going out of his way to be polite to him, as Lord Manister was doing this morning. She divined that politeness from a nobleman was not less gratifying to Herbert because he happened to have maligned the nobleman with much industry. Herbert's modest desire was to be treated as an equal by all men, and he was now being treated as an equal by a lord. This was all he required to make him reasonably civil, even to Lord Manister. When Manister asked him, almost deferentially, whether the mare could be taken in the photograph, he offered his lordship a place in it too, the offer being declined, but not without many thanks.

"I'm going to help take it," Manister laughed. "Mind you don't move, Luttrell. I'm going to help your sister. Hadn't you better come too, and leave my man alone in his glory?"

Herbert replied that he would take off the cap or do anything they liked. So the three went down into the meadow, and some infamous negatives resulted later. At the time care seemed to be taken by the photographers, while Lord Manister stood at a little distance, laughing a good deal. He was pressed to stand in the foreground, but not by Christina, and he steadily refused. The conciliation of his enemy seemed assured without that, though he did think of something else to make it doubly sure.

"By the way, Luttrell," he said as the camera was being packed away, "you're a cricketer to a certainty—you're an Australian."

"I'm very fond of it," the Australian replied, "but I haven't played over here; I've never had the slant."

"Well, we play a bit; come over and practice with us."

Herbert thanked him, declaring that he should like nothing better.

"Lord Manister is a great cricketer," Christina observed.

"Come over and practice," repeated his lordship cordially. "The ground isn't at all bad, considering it was only made last winter, and there's a professor to bowl to you. We have some matches coming on presently. Perhaps we might find a place for you."

This was the one thing Lord Manister said which came within measurable distance of offending the touchy Herbert. A minute later they had parted company.

"They *might* find a place for me," Herbert repeated as he and Tiny turned toward the village, while Lord Manister drove off in the opposite direction, with another slightly ornamental sweep of his hat. "Might they, indeed! I wouldn't take it. My troubles about their matches! But I could enjoy a practice."

"He said he would send over for you next time they do practice."

Those had been Lord Manister's last words.

"He did. He is improved. He's a sportsman, after all. It was decent of him to send back the trap for me. But I didn't want to get in—I was jolly scotty with myself for getting in. I say, Tiny!"

"Well?"

He had her by the arm.

"I don't ask any questions. I don't want to know a single thing. I hope he went down on his knees for his sins; I hope you gave him fits! But look here, Tiny: I won't say a word about this inside if you'd rather I didn't."

"I'd rather you did," Tiny said at once. "There's nothing to hide. But—you can be a dear, good boy when you like, Herbs!"

"Can I? Then you can be offended if you like—but he's on the job now if he never was in his life before!"

"I won't say I hope he isn't," Tiny whispered.

So she was not offended.

CHAPTER VII.
THE SHADOW OF THE HALL.

Such was Christina's first meeting with Lord Manister in his own county. It occurred while his mother's invitation was exhilarating so many homes, and on the day when the Mundham mail bag would not hold the first draught of prompt replies. Until the garden party itself, however, no one at the rectory saw any more of Lord Manister, who had gone for a few days to the Marquis of Wymondham's place in Scotland, where he shot dreadfully on the Twelfth and was otherwise in queer form, considering that Miss Garth was also one of the guests. But under all the circumstances it is not difficult to imagine Manister worried and unhappy during this interval; which, on the other hand, remained in the minds of the people at the rectory, Christina included, as the pleasantest part of their month there.

Not that they suspected this at the time. Mrs. Erskine especially found these days a little slow. Having knowledge of Lord Manister's whereabouts, she was impatient for his return, and the more so because Christina seemed to have forgotten his existence. Christina was indeed puzzling, and on one embarrassing occasion, which with some girls would have led to a scene, she puzzled Ruth more than ever. Ruth tried to follow her presumptive example, and to put aside the thought of Lord Manister for the time being. Her consolation meanwhile was the lively *camaraderie* between Christina and Erskine, wherein Erskine's wife took a delight for which we may forgive her much.

"How well you two get on!" she would say gladly to each of them.

"He's a man and a brother," Tiny would reply.

To which Ruth was sure to say tenderly: "It's sweet of you, dear, to look upon him as a brother.

"Ah, but don't you forget that he's a man, and not my brother really, but just the very best of pals!" Tiny said once. "That's the beauty of him. He's the only man who ever talked sense to me right through from the beginning, so he's something new. He's the only man I ever liked without having the least desire to flirt with him, if you particularly want to know! And I don't believe his being my brother-in-law has anything to do with that," added the girl reflectively; "it would have been the same in any case. What's better still, he's the only man who ever understood me, my dear."

"He's very clever, you see," observed Ruth slyly, but also in all seriousness.

"That's the worst of him; he makes you feel your ignorance."

"I assure you, Tiny, he thinks *you* very clever."

"So you're crackin'!" laughed Tiny; and as the old bush slang filled her mouth unbidden, the smell of a hot wind at Wallandoon came into her nostrils; and there seemed no more to be said.

But that last assurance of Ruth's was still ringing in her ears when her thoughts got back from the bush. She did not believe a word of it. Yet it was more or less true. Nor was Erskine far wrong in any opinion he had expressed to his wife concerning Christina, of whom, perhaps, he had said even less than he thought.

She was not, indeed, to be called an intellectual girl, in these days least of all. That was her misfortune, or otherwise, as you happen to think. Intellectual possibilities, however, she possessed: raw brain with which much might have been done. Not much can be done by a governess on a station in the back-blocks. Merely in curing the girls of the twang of Australia, more successfully than of its slang, and in teaching Tiny to sing rather nicely, the governess at Wallandoon had done wonders. But gifts that were of more use to Christina were natural, such as the quick perception, the long memory, and the ready tongue with which she defended the doors of her mind, so that few might guess the poverty of the store within. Nor had the governess been able to add much to that store. The liking for books had not come to Christina at Wallandoon; but in Melbourne she had taken to reading, and had reveled in a deal of trash; and now in England she read whatever Erskine put in her hands, and honestly enjoyed most of it, with the additional relish of being proud of her enjoyment. Erskine thought her discriminating, too; but converts to good books are apt to flatter the saviors of their taste, and perhaps her brother-in-law was a poor judge of the girl's judgment. He liked her for finding *Colonel Newcome's* life more touching than his death, and for placing the *Colonel* second to *Dr. Primrose* in the order of her gods after reading "The Vicar of Wakefield." He was delighted with her confession that she should "love to be loved by Clive Newcome," while her defense of *Miss Ethel*, which was vigorous enough to betray a fellow-feeling, was interesting at the time, and more so later, when there was occasion to remember it. Similar interest attached to another confession, that she had long envied *Œnone* and *Elaine* "because they were really in love." She seemed to have mixed some good poetry with the bad novels that had contented her in Melbourne. Two more books which she learned to love now were "Sesame and Lilies" and "Virginibus Puerisque." It was Erskine Holland's privilege to put each into her hands for the first time, and perhaps she never pleased him quite so much as when she said: "It makes me think less of myself; it has made me horribly unhappy; but if they were going to hang me in the morning I would sit up all night to read it again!" That was her grace after "Sesame and Lilies."

"Why don't you make Ruth read too?" she asked him once, quite idly, when they had been talking about books.

"She has a good deal to think about," Erskine replied after a little hesitation. "She's too busy to read."

"Or too happy," suggested Tiny.

Mr. Holland made a longer pause, looking gratefully at the girl, as though she had given him a new idea, which he would gladly entertain if he could. "I wonder whether that's possible?" he said at last.

"I'm sure it is. Ruth is so happy that books can do nothing for her; the happy ones show her no happiness so great as her own, and she thinks the sad ones stupid. The other day, when I insisted on reading her my favorite thing in 'Virginibus——'"

"What is your favorite thing?" interrupted Erskine.

"'El Dorado'—it's the most beautiful thing you have put me on to yet, of its size. I could hardly see my way through the last page—I can't tell you why—only because it was so beautiful, I think, and so awfully true! But Ruth saw nothing to cry over; I'm not sure that she saw much to admire; and that's all because you have gone and made her so happy."

For some minutes Erskine looked grim. Then he smiled.

"But aren't you happy too, Tiny?"

"I'm as happy as I deserve to be. That's good enough, isn't it?"

"Quite. You must be as happy as you're pleased to think Ruth."

"Well, then, I'm not. I should like to be some good in the world, and I'm no good at all!"

"I am sorry to see it take you like that," said Erskine gravely. "I wouldn't have thought this of you, Tiny!"

"Ah, there are many things you wouldn't think of me," remarked Tiny. She spoke a little sadly, and she said no more. And this time her sudden silence came from no vision of the bush, but from what she loved much less—a glimpse of herself in the mirror of her own heart.

There was one thing, certainly, that none of them would have thought of her; for she never told them of her little quiet meddlings in the village. But I could tell you. Pleasant it would be to write of what she did for Mrs. Clapperton (who certainly seemed to have been unfairly treated) and of the memories that lived after her in more cottages than one. But you are to see her as they did who saw most of her, and to remember that nothing is more delightful than being kind to the grateful poor, especially when one is privately depressed. Little was ever known of the liberties taken by Christina's generosity, and nothing shall be recorded here. She must stand or fall without that, as in the eyes of her friends. Suffice it that she did amuse herself in this way on the sly, and found it good for restoring her vanity, which was suffering secretly all this time. She would have been the last to take credit for any good she may have done in Essingham. She knew that it wiped out nothing, and also that it made her happier than she would have been otherwise. For though a worse time came later, even now she was not comfortable in her heart. And she had by no means forgotten the existence of Lord Manister, as someone feared.

Ruth, however, put her own conversation under studious restraint during these days, many of which passed without any mention of Lord Minister's name at the rectory. The distracting proximity of his stately home was apparently forgotten in this peaceful spot. But the wife of one clerical neighbor, a Mrs. Willoughby, who accompanied her husband when he came to play lawn tennis with Mr. Holland, and indeed wherever the poor man went, cherished a grudge against the young nobleman's family, of which she made no secret. It was only natural that this lady should air her grievance on the lawn at Essingham, whence there was a distant prospect of lodge and gates to goad her tongue. Yet, when she did so, it was as though the sun had come out suddenly and thrown the shadow of the hall across the rectory garden.

"As for this garden party," cried Mrs. Willoughby, as it seemed for the benefit of the gentlemen, who had put on their coats, and were handing teacups under the trees, "I consider it an insult to the county. It comes too late in the day to be regarded as anything else. Why didn't they do something when first they came here? They have had the place a year. Why didn't they give a ball in the winter, or a set of dinner parties if they preferred that? Shall I tell you why, Mr. Holland? It was because the general election was further off then, and it hadn't occurred to them to put up Lord Manister for the division."

"They haven't been here a year, my dear, by any means," observed Mrs. Willoughby's husband; "and as for dinner parties, we, at any rate, have dined with them."

"Well, I wouldn't boast about it," answered Mrs. Willoughby, who had a sharp manner in conversation, and a specially staccato note for her husband. "We dined with them, it is true; I suppose they thought they must do the civil to a neighboring rector or two. But as their footman had the insolence to tell our coachman, Mrs. Holland, they considered things had reached a pretty pass when it came to dining the country clergy!'"

"Their footman considered," murmured Mr. Willoughby.

"He was repeating what he had heard at table," the lady affirmed, as though she had heard it herself. "They had made a joke of it—before their servants.

So they don't catch me at their garden party, which is to satisfy our social cravings and secure our votes. I don't visit with snobs, Mrs. Holland, for all their coronets and Norman blood—of which, let me tell you, they haven't one drop between them. Who was the present earl's great-grandfather, I should like to know? He never had one; they are not only snobs but upstarts, the Dromards."

"At any rate," Mr. Holland said mildly, "they can't gain anything by being civil to *us*. We don't represent a single vote. We are here for one calendar month."

"Ah, it is wise to be disinterested here and there," rejoined Mrs. Willoughby, whose sharpness was not merely vocal; "it supplies an instance, and that's worth a hundred arguments. Now I shouldn't wonder, Mr. Holland, if they didn't go out of their way to be quite nice to you. I shouldn't wonder a bit. It would advertise their disinterestedness. But wait till you meet them in Piccadilly."

"Mrs. Willoughby is a cynic," laughed Erskine, turning to the clergyman, whose wife swallowed her tea complacently with this compliment to sweeten it. To so many minds a charge of cynicism would seem to imply that intellectual superiority which is cheap at the price of a moral defect.

Now Erskine had a lawn tennis player staying with him for the inside of this week; and the lawn tennis player was a fallen cricketer, who had played against the Eton eleven when young Manister was in it; and he ventured to suggest that the division might find a worse candidate. "He was a nice enough boy then," said he, "and I recollect he made runs; he's a good fellow still, from all accounts."

"From all *my* accounts," retorted Mrs. Willoughby, refreshed by her tea, "he's a very fast one!"

Erskine's friend had never heard that, though he understood that Manister had fallen off in his cricket; he had not seen the young fellow for years, nor did he think any more about him at the moment, being drawn by Herbert into cricket talk, which stopped his ears to the general conversation just as this became really interesting.

"That reminds me," Mrs. Willoughby exclaimed, turning to Ruth. "Was Lord Manister out in Australia in your time?"

Ruth said "No," rather nervously, for Mrs. Willoughby's manner alarmed her. "I was married just before he came out," she added; "as a matter of fact, our steamers crossed in the canal."

"Well, you know what a short time he stayed there, for a governor's aid-de-camp?"

"Only a few months, I have heard. Do let me give you another cup of tea, Mrs. Willoughby!"

"Now I wonder if you know," pursued this lady, having cursorily declined more tea, "how he came to leave so suddenly?"

Poor Mrs. Holland shook her head, which was inwardly besieged with impossible tenders for a change of subject. No one helped her: Tiny had perhaps already lost her presence of mind; Erskine did not understand; the other two were not listening. Ruth could think of no better expedient than a third cup for Christina; as she passed it her own hand trembled, but venturing to glance at her sister's face, she was amazed to find it not only free from all sign of self-consciousness or of anxiety, but filled with unaffected interest. For this was the occasion on which Christina's coolness quite baffled Ruth, who for her part was preparing for a scene.

"Shall I tell you?" asked Mrs. Willoughby.

"Do," said Christina, to whom the well-informed lady at once turned.

"He formed an attachment out there, Miss Luttrell! He could only get out of it by fleeing the country; so he fled. You look as though you knew all about it," she added (making Ruth shudder), for the girl had smiled knowingly.

"About which?" asked Tiny.

"What! Were there more affairs than one?"

"Some people said so."

Mrs. Willoughby glanced around her with a glittering eye, and was sorry to notice that two of her hearers were not listening. "That is just what I expected," she informed the other four. "If you tell me that Melbourne became too hot to hold him I shall not be surprised."

"Melbourne made rather a fuss about him," replied Christina in an excusing tone that pierced Ruth's embarrassment and pricked to life her darling hopes. "He was not greatly to blame."

"But he broke the poor girl's heart. I should blame him for that, to say the least of it."

"You surprise me," said Christina gravely; "I thought that people at home never blamed each other for anything they did in the colonies? Over here you are particular, I know; but I thought it was correct not to be too particular when out there. Your writers come out: we treat them like lords, and then they do nothing but abuse us; your lords come out: we treat them like princes, and, you see, they break our hearts. Of course they do! We expect it of them. It's all we look for in the colonies."

"You are not serious, Miss Luttrell," said Mrs. Willoughby in some displeasure. "To my mind it is a serious thing. It seems a sad thing, too, to me. But I may be old-fashioned; the present generation would crack jokes across an open grave, as I am well aware. Yet there isn't much joke in a young girl having her heart broken by such as Lord Manister, is there? And that's what literally happened, for my friend Mrs. Foster-Simpson knows all about it. She knows all about the Dromards—to her cost!"

"Ah, we know the Foster-Simpsons; they called on us last year," remarked Erskine, who devoutly trusted that they would not call again. His amusement at Christina hardly balanced his weariness of Mrs. Willoughby, and he took off his coat as he spoke.

"Does your friend know the poor girl's name, Mrs. Willoughby?" Tiny asked when the men had gone back to the court; and her tone was now as sympathetic as could possibly be desired.

"I'm sorry to say she does not; it's the one thing she has been unable to find out," said Mrs. Willoughby naïvely. "Perhaps you could tell me, Miss Luttrell?"

"Perhaps I could," said Christina, smiling, as she rose to seek a ball which had been hit into the churchyard. "Only, you see, I don't know which of them it was. It wouldn't be fair to give you a list of names to guess from, would it?"

Fortunately Mrs. Willoughby put no further questions to Ruth, who was intensely thankful. "For," as she told Christina afterward, "*I* was on pins and needles the whole time. I never did know anyone like you for keeping cool under fire!"

"It depends on the fire," Tiny said. "Mrs. Willoughby went off by accident, and luckily she was not pointing at anybody."

"And I'm glad she did, now it's over!" exclaimed Ruth. "Don't you see that I was quite right about your name? So now you need have no more qualms about the garden party."

"Perhaps I've had no qualms for some time; perhaps I've known you were right."

"Since when? Since—since you saw Lord Manister?"

Tiny nodded.

"Do you mean to say you talked about it?" Ruth whispered in delicious awe.

"I mustn't tell you what *he* talked about. He was as nice as he could be—though I should have preferred to find him less beautifully dressed in the country; but I always felt that about him. I am sure, however, of one thing: he was no more to blame than—I was. I have always felt this about him, too."

"Tiny, dear, if only I could understand you!"

"If only you could! Then you might help me to understand myself."

CHAPTER VIII.
"COUNTESS DROMARD AT HOME."

The hall gates were plain enough from the rectory lawn, but plainer still from the steps whence, on the afternoon of the garden party, Mr. Holland watched them from under the brim of the first hard hat he had worn for a fortnight. He was ready, while the ladies were traditionally late, but he did not lose patience; he was too much entertained in watching the hall gates and the hedgerow that hid the road leading up to them. Vehicles were filing along this road in a procession which for the moment was continuous. Erskine could see them over the hedge, and it was difficult to do so without sharing some opinions which Mrs. Willoughby had expressed regarding the comprehensive character of the social measure taken not before it was time by the noble family within those gates. There were county clergymen driving themselves in ill-balanced dogcarts, and county townspeople in carriages manifestly hired, and county bigwigs—as big as the Dromards themselves—in splendid equipages, with splendid coachmen and horseflesh the most magnificent. Greater processional versatility might scarcely be seen in southwestern suburbs on Derby Day; and the low phaeton which he himself was about to contribute to the medley made Erskine laugh.

"We should follow the next really swagger turnout—we should run behind it," he suggested to the girls when at length they appeared; and Ruth took him seriously.

"No, get in front of them," said Herbert, who was lounging on the steps, in dirty flannels which Erskine envied him. "Get in front of them and slow down. That'd be the sporting thing to do! They couldn't pass you in the drive. It would do 'em good."

However, the procession was not without gaps, and to Ruth's satisfaction they found themselves in rather a wide one. As they drove through those august gates a parson's dogcart was rounding a curve some distance ahead, but nothing was in sight behind. Ruth sat beside her husband, who drove. She looked rather demure, but very charming in her little matronly bonnet; her costume was otherwise somewhat noticeably sober, and certainly she had never felt more sensibly the married sister than now, as she glanced at Christina with furtive anxiety, but open admiration. Tiny was neatly dressed in white, and her hat was white also. "Do you know why I wear a white hat?" she asked Erskine on the way; but her question proved merely to be an impudent adaptation of a very disreputable old riddle, and beyond this she was unusually silent during the short drive. Yet she seemed not only self-possessed, but inwardly at her ease. She sat on the little seat in front, often turning round to gaze ahead, and her curiosity and interest were very frank and natural. So were her admiration of the park, her anxiety to see the house itself, and even her wonder at the great length of the drive, which ran alongside the cricket field, and then bent steadily to the left. When at last the low red-brick pile became visible, Gallow Hill was seen immediately behind it, which surprised Christina; the lawn in front was alive with people, which put her on her mettle; and the inspiriting outburst of a military band at that moment forced from her an admission of the pleasure and excitement which had been growing upon her for some minutes.

"I like this!" she exclaimed. "This is first-rate England!"

Countess Dromard stood on the edge of the lawn at the front of the house, and apparently the carriages were unloading at this side of the drive. Ruth whispered hurriedly that she was sure they were, but she was not so sure in reality, and she now saw the disadvantage of arriving in a wide gap, which deprives the inexperienced of their lawful cue. She was quite right, however, and when some minutes elapsed before the arrival of another carriage to interrupt the charming little conversation Ruth had with Lady Dromard, the good of the gap became triumphantly apparent. The countess was very kind indeed. She was a tall, fine woman, with whom the shadows of life had scarce begun to lengthen to the eye; her face was not only handsome, but wonderfully fresh, and she had a trick of lowering it as she chatted with Ruth, bending over her in a way which was comfortable and almost motherly from the first. She had heard of Mrs. Holland, whom she was glad to meet at last, and of whom she now hoped to see something more. Ruth observed that they had the rectory only till September; she was sorry her time was so short. Lady Dromard very flatteringly echoed her sorrow, and also professed an envious admiration for the rectory, which she described as idyllic. That was practically all. What was said of the weather hardly counted; and a repetition of her ladyship's hopes of seeing something more of Mrs. Holland and her party was not worth remembering, according to Erskine, who declared that this meant nothing at all.

Ruth, however, was not likely to forget it; though she treasured just as much the memory of a certain glance which she had caught the countess leveling at her sister. She thought that other eyes also were attracted by the white-robed Tiny, and the smooth-shaven turf was air to Ruth's tread as she marched off with her husband and that cynosure. Nor was her satisfaction decreased when the first person they came across chanced to be no other than Mrs. Willoughby. This meeting was literally the unexpected treat that Ruth pronounced it to be, for the clergyman's wife was smiling in a manner which showed that she had witnessed the countess' singular civility to her friend.

"Yes, I'm here after all," said Mrs. Willoughby grimly. "Henry made me very angry by insisting on coming, but of course I wasn't going to let him come alone. I hope you think he looks happy now he's here!" (Mr. Willoughby and a brother rector might have been hatching dark designs against their bishop, who was himself present, judging by their looks.) "*I* call him the picture of misery. Well, Mrs. Holland, I hope you are gratified at your reception! Oh, it was quite gushing, I assure you; we have all been watching. But wait till you meet them in Piccadilly, my dear Mrs. Holland."

Mrs. Holland left the reply to her husband, who, however, contented himself with promising Mrs. Willoughby a telegraphic report of the proceedings at that meeting, if it ever took place.

"Ah, there won't be much to report," said that redoubtable woman; "they won't look at you. But I shouldn't be surprised to see them make a deal of you in the country, if you let them."

It did not seem conducive to the enjoyment of the afternoon to prolong the conversation with Mrs. Willoughby. The party of three wandered toward the band, admiring the scarlet coats of the bandsmen against the dark green of the shrubbery, and their bright brass instruments flaming in the sun. The music also was of much spirit and gayety, and it was agreed that a band was an immense improvement to a rite of this sort. Then these three, who, after all, knew very few people present, followed the example of others, and made a circuit of the house, in high good humor. But Tiny found herself between two conversational fires, for Ruth would compel her to express admiration for the premises, which might have been taken for granted, while Erskine called her attention to the people, who were much more entertaining to watch. As they passed a table devoted to refreshments, at which a large lady was being waited upon very politely by a small boy in a broad collar, they overheard one of those scraps of conversation which amuse at the moment.

"So you're a Dromard boy, are you?" the lady was saying. "I've never seen you before. What Dromard boy are *you*, pray?"

"My name's Douglas."

"Oh! So you're the Honorable Douglas Dromard, are you?"

The boy handed her an ice without answering as the three passed on.

"I said you'd see and hear some queer things," whispered Mr. Holland; "but you won't hear anything much finer than that. The woman is Mrs. Foster-Simpson; her husband's a solicitor, and may be the Conservative agent, if his wife doesn't disqualify him. She professes to know all about the Dromards, as you heard the other day. You can guess the kind of knowledge. Even the boy snubs her. Yet mark him. The mixture of politeness and contempt was worth noticing in a small boy like that. There's a little nobleman for you!"

"No, a little Englishman," said Tiny. "Now that's a thing I do envy you—your schoolboys, your little gentlemen! We don't grow them so little in the colonies; we don't know how."

They were walking on a majestic terrace in the shadow of the red-brick house, their figures mirrored in each mullioned window as they passed it.

"I call Lord Manister the luckiest young man in England," Ruth exclaimed during a pause between the other two. "To think that all this will be his!"

"It rather reminds me of Hampton Court on this side," remarked Tiny indifferently.

"And it's by no means their only place, you know; there are others they never use, are there not, Erskine?—to say nothing of all those squares and streets in town!"

But Erskine sounded the thick sibilant of silence as they passed a shabby looking person with a slouching walk and a fair beard.

"I wonder how *he* got here?" Tiny murmured next moment.

"He has a better right than most of us."

"What do you mean, Erskine?"

"Well, it's the earl."

"Earl Dromard? I should have guessed his gardener!"

"No, that's the earl. Old clothes are his special fancy in the country. It's his particular form of side, so they say."

"Well," said Tiny, "I prefer it to his son's, which has always appeared to me to be the other extreme."

"I am sure Lord Manister is not over-dressed," remonstrated Ruth, with her usual alacrity in defense of his lordship.

"No, that's the worst of him," answered her sister. "There is nothing to find fault with, ever; that's what makes one think he employs his intellect on the study of his appearance."

They had seen Lord Manister in the distance. Presumably he had not seen them, but he might have done so; and Ruth supposed it was the doubt that made her sister speak of him more captiously than usual. But the criticism was not utterly unfair, as Ruth might presently have seen for herself; for as they came back to the front of the house, Lord Manister detached himself from a group, and approached them with the suave smile and the slight flourish of the hat which were two of his tricks. Christina asked afterward if the flourish was not dreadfully continental, but she was told that it was merely up to date, like the hat itself. At the time, however, she introduced Lord Manister to her sister Mrs. Erskine Holland, and to Mr. Holland, taking this liberty with charming grace and tact, yet with a becoming amount of natural shyness. Manister, for one, was pleased with the introduction on all grounds. From the first, however, he addressed himself to the married lady, speaking partly of the surrounding country, for which Ruth could not say too much, and partly of Melbourne, which enabled him to return her compliments. His manner was eminently friendly and polite. Discovering that they had not yet been in the house for tea, he led the way thither, and through a throng of people in the hall, and so into the dining room. Here he saved the situation from embarrassment by making himself equally attentive to another party. To Ruth, however, Lord Manister's civility was still sufficiently marked, while he asked her husband whether he was a cricketer; and this reminded him of Herbert, for whom he gave Miss Luttrell a message. He said they had just arranged some cricket for the last week of the month; he thought they would be glad of Miss Luttrell's brother in one or two of the matches. But he seemed to fear that most of the teams were made up; his young brother was arranging everything. Christina gathered that in any case they would be glad to see Herbert at the nets any afternoon of the following week, more especially on the Monday. Lord Manister made a point of the message, and also of the cricket week, "when," he said, "you must all turn up if it's fine." And those were his last words to them.

"I see you know my son," said the countess in her kindliest manner as Ruth thanked her for a charming afternoon.

"My sister met him the other day at Lady Almeric's," replied Ruth, "and before that in Australia."

"I knew Lord Manister in Melbourne," added Tiny with freedom.

"Do you mean to tell me you are Australians?" said Lady Dromard in a tone that complimented the girls at the expense of their country. "Then you must certainly come and see me," she added cordially, though her surprise was still upon her. "I am greatly interested in Australia since my son was there. I feel I have a welcome for all Australians—you welcomed him, you know!"

Christina afterward expressed the firm opinion that Lady Dromard had said this rather strangely, which Ruth as firmly denied. Tiny was accused of an imaginative self-consciousness, and the accusation provoked a blush, which Ruth took care to remember. Certainly, if the countess had spoken queerly, the queerness had escaped the one person who was not on the lookout for something of the kind; Erskine Holland had perceived nothing but her ladyship's condescension, which had been indeed remarkable, though Erskine still told his wife to expect no further notice from that quarter.

"And I'm selfish enough to hope you'll get none, my dears," he said to the girls that evening as they sauntered through the kitchen garden after dinner; "because for my part I'd much rather not be noticed by them. We were not intended to take seriously anything that was said this afternoon; honey was the order of the day for all comers—and can't you imagine them wiping their foreheads when we were all gone? I only hope they wiped us out of their heads! We're much happier as we are. I'm not rabid, like Mrs. Willoughby; but she prophesied a very possible experience, when all's said and done, confound her! I have visions of Piccadilly myself. And seriously, Ruth, you wouldn't like it if you became friendly with these people here and they cut you in town; no more should I. I think you can't be too careful with people of that sort; and if they ask us again I vote we don't go; but they won't ask us any more, you may depend upon it."

"I don't depend upon it, all the same," replied Ruth, with some spirit. "Lady Dromard was most kind; and as for Lord Manister, *I* was enchanted with him."

"Were you?" Tiny said, feeling vaguely that she was challenged.

"I was; I thought him unaffected and friendly, and even simple. I am sure he is simple-minded! I am also sure that you won't find another young man in his position who is better natured or better hearted——"

"Or better mannered—or better dressed! You are quite right; he is nearly perfect. He is rather too perfect for me in his manners and appearance; I should like to untidy him; I should like to put him in a temper. Lord Manister was never in a temper in his life; he's nicer than most people—but he's too nice altogether for me!"

"You knew him rather well in Melbourne?" said Erskine, eyeing his sister-in-law curiously; her face was toward the moon, and her expression was set and scornful.

"Very well indeed," she answered with her erratic candor.

"I might have guessed as much that time in town. I say, if we meet *him* in Piccadilly we may score off Mrs. Willoughby yet! Wait till we get back——"

"All right; only don't let us wait out here," Ruth interrupted—"or Tiny and I may have to go back in our coffins!"

CHAPTER IX.
MOTHER AND SON.

A clever man is not necessarily an infallible prophet; and the clever man who is married may well preserve an intellectual luster in the eyes of his admirer by never prophesying at all. But should he take pleasure in predicting the thing that is openly deprecated at the other side of the hearth, let him see to it that his prediction comes true, for otherwise he has whetted a blade for his own breast, from whose justifiable use only an angel could abstain. There was no angel in the family which had been brought up on Wallandoon Station, New South Wales. When, within the next three days, Ruth received a note from Lady Dromard inviting them all to dinner at a very early date, she did not fail to prod Erskine as he deserved. But her thrust was not malignant; nor did she give vexatious vent to her own triumph, which was considerable.

"You are a very clever man," she merely told him, and with the relish of a wife who can say this from her heart; "but you see, you're wrong for once. Lady Dromard *did* mean what she said. She wants us all to dine there on Friday evening, when, as it happens, we have no other engagement; and really I don't see how we can refuse."

"You mean that you would like to get out of it if you could?" her husband said.

"You don't need to be sarcastic," remarked Ruth with a slight flush. "Who wants to get out of it?"

"I thought perhaps you did, my dear; to tell you the truth, I rather hoped so."

"You don't want to go!"

"I can't say I jump."

Ruth colored afresh.

"I have no patience with you, Erskine! Nobody is dying to go; but I own I can't see any reason against going, nor any excuse for stopping away; and considering what you yourself said about going to the garden party, dear, I must say I think you're rather inconsistent."

Holland gazed down into the flushed, frowning face, that frowned so seldom, and flushed so prettily. Always an undemonstrative husband, very properly he had been more so than ever since others had been staying in the house. But neither of those others was present now, and rather suddenly he stooped and kissed his wife.

"There is no reason, and there would be no excuse; so you are quite right," he said kindly. "It's only that one has a constitutional dislike to being taken up—and dropped. I have visions of all that. I'm afraid Mrs. Willoughby has poisoned my mind; we will go, and let us hope it'll prove an antidote."

They went, and that dinner party was not the formidable affair it might have been; as Lady Dromard herself said, most graciously, it was not a dinner party at all. Ten, however, sat down, of whom four came from the rectory; for Herbert had been over to practice at the nets, and was fairly satisfied with his treatment on that occasion, which accounted for his presence on this. The only other guests were an inevitable divine and his wife. The earl was absent. As if to conserve Christina's impression of the old clothes in which, as the natives said, his lordship "liked himself," Earl Dromard had left for London rather suddenly that morning. Lord Manister filled his place impeccably, with Ruth at her best on his right. Herbert was less happy with Lady Mary Dromard, a very proud person, who could also be very rude in the most elegant manner. But Christina fell to the jolliest scion of the house, Mr. Stanley Dromard; and this pair mutually enjoyed themselves.

Young in every way was the Honorable Stanley Dromard. He had just left Eton, where he had been in the eleven, like his brother before him; he was to go into residence at Trinity in October. With a quantum of gentlemanly interest he heard that Miss Luttrell's brother was also going up to Cambridge next term; but not to Trinity. Said Mr. Dromard, "Your brother's a bit of a cricketer, too; he came over for a knock the other day; he means to play for us next week, if we're short, doesn't he?" Christina fancied so. Mr. Dromard said "Good!" with some emphasis, and Herbert's name dropped out of the conversation. This became Anglo-Australian, as it was sure to, and led to some of those bold comparisons for which Christina was generally to be trusted; but the bolder they were, the more Mr. Dromard enjoyed them, for the girl glittered in his eyes. He was a delightfully appreciative youth, if easily amused, and his laughter sharpened Tiny's wits. She shone consciously, but yet calmly, and made a really remarkable impression upon her companion, without once meeting Lord Manister's glance, which rested on her sometimes for a second.

So the flattering attentions of young Dromard were not terminated, but merely interrupted, by the flight of the ladies. When the men followed them to the drawing room the younger son shot to Miss Luttrell's side with the fine regardlessness of nineteen, and furthered their friendship by divulging the Mundham plans for the following week. The cricket was to begin on the Tuesday. The men were coming the day before: half the Eton eleven, Tiny understood, and some older young fellows of Manister's standing. The first two were to be two-day matches against the county and a Marylebone team.

The Saturday's match would be between Mundham Hall and another scratch eleven, "and that's when we may want your brother, Miss Luttrell," added Mr. Dromard, "though we *might* want him before. Our team has been made up some time, but somebody is sure to have some other fixture for Saturday."

"I think he may like to play," said Christina.

Mr. Dromard seemed a little surprised.

"It's a jolly ground," he remarked, "and there will be some first-rate players."

"I am sure he would like a game on your ground," Christina went so far as to say.

"Do you dance, Miss Luttrell?" asked the young man, after a pause.

"When I get the chance," said Christina.

He gazed at her a moment, and could imagine her dancing—with him.

"Suppose we were to do something of the kind here one evening between the matches; would you come?"

"If I got the chance," said Christina.

Dromard considered what he was saying. "We ought to have a dance," he added in a doubtful tone, as though the need were greater than the chance; "we really ought. But I don't suppose we shall; nothing is arranged, you see."

"You needn't hedge, Mr. Dromard," said the girl, smiling.

"Eh?"

"I shan't expect an invitation!"

She nodded knowingly as he blushed; but he had the great merit of being easily amused, and with another word she made him merry and at ease again. Not unreasonably, perhaps, a casual spectator might have suspected these two of a mild but immediate flirtation. Stanley, however, was at a safe and privileged age, and no eye was on him but his brother's. Lord Manister gave the impression of being a rather dignified person in his own home, but he was doing his gracious duty by the guests, none of whom seemed especially to occupy his attention, while he was reasonably polite to all. It was he, too, who at length suggested to Lady Dromard that Miss Luttrell would probably sing something if she were asked.

So Christina sang something—it hardly matters what. Her song was not a classic, neither was it grossly popular. It was a pleasant song, pleasantly sung, and the entire absence of pretentiousness and of affectation in the song and the singing was more noticeable than the positive excellence of either. The girl had no greater voice than one would have expected of so small a person, but what she had was in keeping. Lady Dromard, however, had a more sensitive appreciation of good taste than of good music, and she asked for more. Christina sang successively something of Lassen's, and then "Last Night," taking the English words in each case. She played her own accompaniments, and felt little nervousness until her last song was finished, when it certainly startled her to find Lady Dromard standing at her side.

"Thank you!" said the countess with considerable enthusiasm. "You sing delightfully, and you sing delightful songs. You must have been very well taught."

"Mostly in the bush," said Christina truthfully.

"You come from the bush?"

"But you had some lessons in Melbourne," put in Ruth, who was visibly delighted.

"Oh, yes, a few," Tiny said, smiling; "as many as I was worth."

"Ah, you shall tell me about Melbourne one day soon," said Lady Dromard to the young girl. "Your sister has promised to come over and watch the cricket. I do hope you will come with her."

Christina expressed her pleasure at the prospect, and, taking the nearest seat, found Lord Manister leaning over the end of the piano and looking down upon her with a rather sardonic smile.

"You haven't looked at me this evening," he said to her under cover of the general conversation, which was now renewed. "May I ask what I have done?"

"Certainly you may ask, Lord Manister," answered the girl with immense simplicity; "but I can't tell you, because I am not aware that you have done anything beyond making us all very happy and at home."

"Well, I'm glad to hear that," said Manister, whose quasi-humorous tone lacked the lightness to deceive; "I was afraid I had offended you."

"Offended me!" cried Christina, with widening eyes and a puzzled look. "When have you seen me to offend me! I haven't seen you since your garden party, and you certainly didn't offend me then—you were awfully nice to us all!"

"Ah, that wasn't seeing you," Lord Manister murmured. "I don't reckon that I've seen you since—the photographs. I had to go to Scotland; I meant to tell you."

"It wouldn't have interested me," said Christina, with a shrug. "It might have interested me if you had said—you were *not* going," she added next moment. Her tone had dropped. She looked at him and smiled.

Her smile stayed with him after she was gone; but from his face you would not have guessed that he was nursing a kind look. She had given him one smile, which made up for many things. But you would have thought, with his people, that he had been suffering the whole evening from acute boredom: you might well have fancied, with Lady Mary, that a remark disparaging Australian women would have met with a grateful response from him. The response it did meet with was anything but grateful to Lady Mary Dromard. It drove her from the room, in which Manister and his mother were presently left alone.

"I think you were just," the countess said critically. "They are pleasant people, and quite all right. The young man is their weak point."

"They always are," her son remarked, rather savagely still. "They're larrikins!"

"The young girl was especially nice, and sang like a lady."

"Ah, you approve of her," said Lord Manister dryly.

"Entirely, I think. Evidently you don't. I only saw you speak to her once, toward the end. Yet she has met you in Australia; I should have recognized that, I think. Now her people," Lady Dromard added tentatively, "will be rather superior, I suppose, as colonials go?"

"Well, they're rich; I suppose that's how colonials go."

For one moment Lady Dromard fancied that the sneer was for the colonials, and it surprised her; the next, she took it to herself, and very meekly for so proud a heart.

"My dear boy!" she murmured indulgently. "Apart from their people, these girls—for the married one is as young as she has any right to be—strike one as fresh, and free, and pleasing. And they are ladies. Am I to believe that the majority out there are like them?"

Manister shrugged his shoulders.

"That's as you please, my dear mother. These people didn't strike me as the only decent ones in Melbourne. I did meet others."

The countess tapped her foot upon the fender, and took counsel with her own reflection in the mirror, for she was standing before the fireplace while her son wandered about the room—her son with the reputation for a childlike devotion to his mother. There had been little of that sort of devotion since his return from Australia. Nothing between them was as it had been before. This bitter coldness had been his domestic manner—his manner with her, of all people—longer than the mother could bear. She knew the reason; she had tried to tell him so; she had tried to speak freely to him of the whole matter—even penitently, if he would. But he had never spoken freely to her; and once he had refused to speak at all, thence or thenceforth. Lady Dromard had made a resolve then which she remembered now.

"Really, Harry, I can't make you out," she said lightly at length. "You knock down the colonials with one hand, and you set them up with the other, as though they were so many ninepins. I am puzzled to know what you really mean, and what you mean satirically. You never used to be satirical, Harry! I should like to know whether you really approve of these people, or whether you don't."

"I do approve of them," said Lord Manister, halting on the rug before his mother. "I won't put it more strongly. But I am glad that you should have seen there are such things as ladies in Australia!"

Their eyes met, and the mother forgot her resolve; for he had raised the subject himself, and for the first time.

"You think of her still!" whispered Lady Dromard.

"Of course I do," returned Manister, roughly; and again he was striding about the room.

Never in her life, perhaps, had the countess received a sharper hurt; for he had refused to see the hand she had reached out to him involuntarily. Yet assuredly Lady Dromard had never spoken in a more ordinary tone than that of her next words, a minute later.

"It occurred to me, Harry, that if we really think of dancing one evening during the cricket week, we might do worse than ask these people from the rectory. You must have girls to dance with. Still, if you think better not, you have only to say so."

"I think it's for you to decide; but, if you ask me, I don't see the least objection to it," said Lord Manister, with a smooth ceremony that had a sharper edge than his rough words. "I'm not sure, however, that they will come every time you ask them."

"Pourquoi?"

"Because they're the most independent people in the world, the Australians."

"It would scarcely touch their independence," said Lady Dromard with careless contempt; "but we can really do without them, and I am glad of your hint, because now I shall not think of asking them."

"Now, my dear mother," cried Lord Manister, no longer either hot or cold, but his old self for once in his anxiety—"you misunderstand me entirely! I'm not great on a dance at all, but if we're to have one we must, as you say, have somebody to dance with; and I *want* you to ask these people."

CHAPTER X.
A THREATENING DAWN.

"I like a dance where you can dance," said Herbert, who was looking at himself in a glass and wondering how long his white tie had been on one side. "It was worth fifty of the swell show you took us to in town, Ruth."

"I am glad you two have enjoyed it so," returned Ruth, with her eye, however, upon her husband. "Of course there's a great difference between a big dance in town and a little one in the country."

Tiny seemed busy. She was tearing her programme into small pieces, and dropping them at her feet, so that when she had gone up to bed it was as though a paper chase had passed through the rectory study, where they had all gathered for a few moments on their return from the dance. Christina, however, was not too preoccupied to chime in on her own note:

"It's like the difference between Riverina and Victoria—there were acres to the sheep instead of sheep to the acre."

Now there was no merit in this speech, but to those who understood it the comparison was apt, and Erskine knew enough of Australia to understand. Moreover, he had taught Tiny to listen for his laugh. So when he made neither sound nor sign the girl felt injured, but remembered that he had been extremely silent on the way home. And he was the first to go upstairs.

"It has bored him," observed Christina.

"He don't like dancing," said Herbert. "He's no sportsman."

"I am afraid he cares for nothing but lawn tennis when he's here," sighed Ruth, who looked a little troubled. "I am afraid he dislikes going out in the country."

They were silent for some minutes before Tiny exclaimed with conviction:

"No; it's the Dromards he dislikes."

And presently they made a move from the room. But on the stairs they met Erskine coming down, having changed his dress suit for flannels; and Ruth followed him back to the study, eying the change with dismay.

"Surely you're not going to sit up at this hour?"

Ruth had raised her glance from his flannels to his face, which troubled her more.

"I'm afraid the fine weather's at an end," Erskine answered crookedly; "it's most awfully close, at any rate. And I want a pipe."

He proceeded to fill one with his back to her.

"Erskine!"

"Well, dear?"

"I won't be 'dear' to you when you're cross with me. I want to know what I have done to vex you."

He had struck a match, and he lit his pipe before answering. Then he said gently enough:

"If you think I'm cross with you I should run away to bed; I certainly don't mean to be."

But he had not turned round.

"You succeed, at any rate! As you seem to wish it, I shall take your advice."

Erskine heard her on the stairs with a twinge in his heart. He went to the door to call her down and be frank with her, but the shutting of her own door checked him. Setting this one ajar, he threw up the window, and stood frowning at the opaque pall that seemed to have been let down behind it like an outer blind. So he remained for some minutes before remembering the easy-chair. No one knew better than Erskine that he had just been unkind to his wife. He was not pleased with her, but he had refused to explain his displeasure when she invited him to do so. There was this difficulty in explaining it—that he knew it to be unreasonable, since the person who had vexed him most was not Ruth, but Christina. And not more reasonable was his disappointment in Christina, as he also knew. Yet the one thing in life not disappointing to him at the moment was his pipe; even the fine weather was most surely at an end.

He was tired of the rectory, which, wet or fair, had no longer either light or shadow of its own, for both were now absorbed in the deepening shadow of the hall. A week ago they had all dined there, now they had been dancing there, and meanwhile the girls had watched one of the matches, and were going to another. Erskine had been opposed to the dance, but the wife had prevailed; he was against their going to another match, but doubtless Ruth would have her way again, for she had shown a tenacity of purpose that surprised him in her, while he was crippled by a conscious lack of logic in his objections. He was not an arbitrary person, and it seemed that Ruth would stop for nothing less than a command where her heart was set; and her sister was with her. The whole trouble was, where their hearts were set.

He tried hard not to think the worst of Tiny, or rather the worst as it seemed to him. To make it easier, he called to mind various things she had said to him at various times concerning Lord Manister, of whom she had seldom failed to make fun. It amused and consoled Erskine to remember the fun; there must be hope for her still. Then he recalled common gossip about Lord Manister and his affairs; and there was hope on that side too. In less than a week the danger would be past, and those two would never see each other again. Consideration of the danger he had in mind, *quá* danger, provoked a smile. Tiny herself would have enjoyed the humor of that, she was so quick to see and to enjoy. But she could appreciate more than a joke, or did she only pretend to like those books? And the soul that shone sometimes in her eyes, did it lie much deeper? She interested Erskine the more because he could not be sure. She was a fascinating study to him, whatever she did or was trying to do. In any case, there was much good in her that he had fathomed, and more was suggested; and the finer the nature, the stronger the contrasts. Now as to contrasts—yet he had never seen that in Australia.

"A penny for your thoughts!"

Ten thousand pounds would not have bought them. It was his wife on the threshold, in a pale pink wrapper.

"My dear! I pictured you asleep hours ago."

"Were you picturing me when I spoke?" Ruth said, with a smile. "I'm not sleepy—and I want to talk to you. May I sit down? An hour more or less makes no difference at this time of the morning."

Erskine rose from the easy-chair in which he had been smoking, and settled his wife in it against her will, and drew the curtains across the open window.

"I'm glad you've come down, Ruth, for I want to speak to you, too. I was a brute to you when I sent you away just now."

"Well, I really think you were; but I know you must have had some reason; so I've come down to have it out and be done with it."

"My dear Ruth!" said Mr. Holland uncomfortably; for was there any call to be frank with her at all? It would hurt; and could it do any good?

"I suppose," pursued Ruth in a tone not perfectly free from defiance, "it's all because we went to this horrid dance! And I'll say I'm sorry we did go, if you like; though why you should have such a down on the Dromards I can't for the life of me imagine."

"My dear girl," said Erskine, smiling now that he had determined not to say everything, "I really have no down on them at all. They're the most amiable family I know, considering who they are. They have a charming place, and they treat you delightfully while you're there. Considering who *we* are, and that we have no root in this soil, I grant you they're particularly kind to us; but don't you think their kindness is just a little trying? I do, though I have nothing against them, personally or otherwise. I am not even a political opponent; if I had a vote for the division young Manister should have it. But I'm not keen on so much notice from them; I've said so before; there's no sense in it!"

"Ah, well, if only you would show me the harm in it!"

"Harm? Heaven forbid there should be any. One finds it a bore, that's all. It's a selfish reason, but it's the truth—I should have had a better time this last week if the Dromards had been far enough!"

"And we should have had a worse—Tiny and I. No, Erskine, I know you better than you think. You're not so selfish as all that; there's some other reason."

Erskine turned away with a shrug, to avoid her glance.

"Something has annoyed you to-night. One of us has behaved badly. Was it Tiny or was it——"

"You?" said Erskine, with a smile. "From what I saw of your behavior, my dear, it was entirely creditable to you as a chaperon. Your face was seventeen, but your air was a frank fifty!"

"Then it was Tiny. I suppose she danced too much with those boys they have staying in the house. I should have thought there was respectability in numbers; I really don't see how *they* could matter."

"They seemed to matter to Manister," remarked Erskine dryly.

Ruth winced, but he had wondered whether she would, or he would never have noticed it.

"Surely you don't think Lord Manister cares who dances with our Tiny?"

The amusement in her tone and manner was cleverly feigned, but instead of deceiving Erskine it spurred him to speak out, after all.

"I hardly like to tell you what I think about Tiny and Lord Manister," he said gravely.

"What on earth do you mean, Erskine?" cried Ruth, reddening. "Now you *must* tell me!"

Erskine temporized, already regretting that he had said so much. "It would hurt your feelings," he warned her grimly.

"Not so much as your silence."

"I wouldn't say it if I didn't look on her as my own sister by this time, and if I didn't think her the best little girl in the world—but one."

Now he spoke tenderly.

"Say it, in any case," said Ruth, who had been uncommonly calm.

"Then I am afraid she is making up to him, if you must know."

"Which is absurd," said Ruth lightly; but in her anxiety to remain cool she forgot to seem surprised; and that was a mistake.

"I wonder if you really think so?" said her husband very quietly. "If you do I can't agree with you; I wish I could."

"You must!" cried Ruth desperately. "Do you know how many dances she gave him to-night?"

Erskine knew only of one; his eyes rested on the remains of her programme lying on the floor in many fragments.

"Well, that one was the lot!" he was informed severely. "And pray did you count how many times she spoke to him the other evening when we dined at the hall?"

"Not often, I grant you; I noticed that."

"Yet you think she is making up to him!"

"It's a strong way of putting it, I know," said Erskine reluctantly; "but really I can't think of any other. I wonder you don't realize that there are more ways of making up to a man than the dead-set method. Can't you see that a far more effective method is a little judicious snubbing and avoiding, which is coquetry? You take my word for it, that's the touch for a man like Manister, who is probably accustomed to everything but being snubbed and avoided. Then you speak of the one dance she gave him. Now I happen to know that they didn't dance it at all; they spent the time under the stars, for it was my misfortune to see them and their misfortune not to see me."

"Well?" whispered Ruth; and though she had never been so dark until now, that whisper would have drawn his lantern to her real hopes and fears.

"I only saw them for an instant: I bolted; so I may easily be wrong; but it struck me that our Tiny was making up for her snubbing and avoiding. It has since occurred to me that they must have known each other rather well in Melbourne—rather better, at any rate, than you have ever led me to suppose."

As a woman's last resource, Ruth aimed a stone at his temper.

"So that's it!" she exclaimed viciously.

"That's what?"

"The secret of your bad temper."

"Well, to be kept in the dark doesn't sweeten a man, certainly," Erskine answered, in a tone, however, that was far from bitter. "Then one can't help feeling disappointed with Tiny; and in this matter—to be frank with you at last—I am just a little disappointed in you too, my dear."

"I always knew you would be," said Ruth dolefully. For her stone had missed, and there was no more fight in her.

"Now don't be a goose. It's only in this one matter, in which—I can't help telling you—I don't think you've been perfectly straight with me."

"Oh, indeed!" cried Ruth, as her spirit made one spurt more. It was the last. The next moment she was weeping.

It annoys most men to make a woman cry. Those who do not become annoyed make impetuous atonement, partly, no doubt, to drown the hooting in their own heart. But Erskine could not feel himself to blame, and though he spoke very kindly, his kindness was too nearly paternal, and he spoke with his elbow on the chimney-piece. He told Ruth not to do that. He pointed out to her that there was no crime in her want of candor concerning her sister's affairs, which were certainly no business of his. Only, if there really had been something between Christina and Lord Manister in Melbourne—if, for instance, Mrs. Willoughby had gossiped unwittingly to Christina about none other than Christina herself—Erskine put it to his wife that she might have done more wisely to place him in a position silently to appreciate such capital jokes. He would have said nothing; but as it was he might easily have said much to imperil the situation; in fact, he had been in a false position all along, more especially at the hall. But that was all. There was really nothing to cry about. Perhaps to give her the fairest opportunity to compose herself, Erskine crossed the room and drew back the curtains to let in the gray morning; for the birds had long been twittering.

But Ruth had been waiting for the touch of his hand, and he had only given her kind words. She looked up, and saw through her tears his form against the gray window, as he shut down the sash. The lamp burnt faintly, and in the two wan lights it was a chamber of misery, in which one could not sit alone. Ruth rose and ran to Erskine, and laid her hands upon his arm.

"It is raining," he said, without looking at her tears. "I knew we were in for a break up of the fine weather."

"Never mind the rain!" Ruth cried piteously, with her face upon his coat. "Will you forgive me now if I tell you everything that I know—everything? It isn't much, because Tiny has been almost as close with me as I have been with you."

"My dear," he said, patting her head at last, and with his arms around her lightly, "you both had a perfect right to be close."

"But suppose I've been at the bottom of the whole thing? Suppose I turn out a horrid little intriguer—what then?"

She waited eagerly, and the pause seemed long.

"Well, you won't have been intriguing for yourself," sighed Erskine—so that her face rose on his breast, as on a wave.

And then, playing nervously with a button of his coat, Ruth confessed all. As she spoke she gathered confidence, but not enough to watch his face. That was turned to the gray morning, and looked as gray as it. The fine weather had indeed broken up, and Essingham had lost its savor for Erskine Holland.

CHAPTER XI.
IN THE LADIES' TENT.

And yet, even at the time she made it, Ruth little dreamt how deeply her confession both galled and revolted her husband. He forgave her very kindly in the end, and that satisfied her lean imagination. Perhaps there was not much to forgive. There was enough, at all events, to trouble Erskine (to whom the best excuse there was for her was the least likely to suggest itself); but the matter soon ceased to trouble Erskine's wife, because his smile was as good-tempered as before. He seemed, indeed, to think no more about it. When Ruth would speak confidentially of her hopes and wishes for Tiny (as though Erskine had been in her confidence all the time), he would chat the matter over with interest, which was the next best thing to sympathy. He had to do this oftener than he liked during the next twenty-four hours; for Ruth really thought that excessive candor now was a more or less adequate atonement for an excessive reserve in the past. Moreover, she genuinely enjoyed talking openly at last of the matter which had concerned her so long and so severely in secret.

"Don't you think he means it?" she asked her husband several times.

"I am afraid he thinks he does," was one of Holland's answers.

"That's your way of admitting it," rejoined Ruth, who could bear his repudiation of her desires for the sake of his assent to her opinion, which Erskine was too honest to withhold. "Of course he means it. Have you noticed how he watches her?"

"I have noticed it once or twice."

"And did you see him watching his mother, the night we dined there, to see what impression Tiny made upon her?"

"So you spotted that!" Erskine said curiously, not having given his wife the credit for such acute perception. "Well, I own that I did, too; and that was worse than his watching Tiny. This is a youth with a well-known weakness for his mamma. She has probably more influence over him than any other body in the world. I am prepared to bet that it was she, and she alone, who whistled him back from Australia. Now though she did it partly by her singing—which, by the way, was rather cheap for our Tiny—there's no doubt at all about the impression Tiny has made upon Lady Dromard; and that's the worst of it."

"The worst of it! as if he was beneath her!" said Ruth mockingly. "Or is it that you think her too terribly beneath him?"

"Tiny," said Erskine, shaking his head, "is beneath no man that I have yet come across."

"Then what can you have against it? Is it that you think she will grow so grand that we shall see no more of her! If so, it shows how much you know of our Tiny. Or do you think him too high and mighty to be honest and true? I don't profess to know much about it," continued Ruth scornfully, being stung to eloquence by his perversity, "but I should have said an honest man and his love might be found in a castle, sometimes, as well as in a cottage!"

"'Hearts just as pure and fair may beat in Belgrave Square as in the lowly air of Seven Dials,'" quoted Erskine, with a laugh. "I grant all that; but if you want to know, my point is that Tiny would be thrown away on Belgrave Square! She is far too funny and fresh, and unlike most of us, to thrive in that fine soil; she would need to be clipped and pruned and trimmed in the image of other people. And that would spoil her. Whatever else she may be, she's more or less original as she stands. She's not a copy now; but she will have to become one in Belgrave Square."

"She *will* have to become one!" cried Ruth, jumping at the change of mood. "Then you think that Tiny means it, too?"

"I am afraid she means to marry him," said Erskine, with a sigh. "I have visions of our Tiny ours no more, but my Lady Manister, and Countess Dromard in due course."

So delighted was Ruth with his opinion on this point that his other opinions had no power to annoy her; and in her joy she told him once more, and with much impulsive feeling, how sorry she was for having kept him in the dark so willfully and so long. She called him an angel of good temper and forbearance, and undertook to reward his generosity by never hiding another thing from him in her life. And she would never, never vex him again, she said—so earnestly that he thought she meant it, as indeed she thought herself, for half a minute.

"But you mean to go to the match to-morrow?" he asked her wistfully.

"Oh, we must—if it's fine. It's the last match of the week; besides, Herbert's going to play."

This was an argument, and Erskine said no more. The chances are that he would have said no more in any case. The following afternoon Ruth drove with Tiny to the match, and with a particularly light heart, because she had not heard another word against the plan. Her one remaining anxiety was lest it might rain before they got to the cricket field.

For the day was one of those dull ones of early autumn when there is little wind, a gray sky, and more than a chance of rain; but none had fallen during the morning, which reduced the chance; while the clouds were high, and occasionally parted by faint rays of sunshine. The ground was so beautiful in itself that it was the greater pity there was no more sun, since, without it, well-kept turf and tall trees are like a sweet face saddened. The trees were the fine elms of that country, and they flanked two sides of the ground; but one missed their shadows, and the foliage had a dingy, lack-luster look in the tame light. On the third side a ha-ha formed a natural "boundary," and the red, spreading house stood aloof on the fourth, giving a touch of welcome warmth to a picture whose highest lights were the white flannels of the players and the canvas tents. The tents were many, and admirably arranged; but one beneath the elms had a side on the ground to itself; and thither drove Mrs. Holland, alighting rather nervously as a groom came promptly to the pony's head, because this was the ladies' tent.

To-day, however, the tent was not formidably full, as it had been when the girls had watched the cricket from it earlier in the week; this was only the Saturday's match. Ruth looked in vain for Lady Dromard, but received a cold greeting from her daughter, Lady Mary, upon whom the guinea stamp was disagreeably fresh and sharp. The sight of Mrs. Willoughby and her friend Mrs. Foster-Simpson on a front seat was a relief at the moment (the sight of anything to nod to is a relief sometimes); but Ruth was discreet enough to sit down behind these ladies, not beside them. She congratulated herself on her presence of mind when she heard the tone and character of some of their comments on the game. It would have done Ruth no good to be seen at the side of loud Mrs. Foster-Simpson or of loquacious Mrs. Willoughby, and it might have done Tiny grave harm. Mrs. Willoughby's husband, who had good-naturedly become eleventh man at the eleventh hour, was conspicuous in the field from his black trousers, clerical wide-awake, and shirt-sleeves of gray flannel. "I hope you admire him," said his wife over her shoulder to Ruth; "I tell him he might as well take a funeral in flannels!"

"Or dine in his surplice," added her friend Mrs. Foster-Simpson in a voice that carried to the back of the tent.

"I just do admire Mr. Willoughby," Ruth said softly; "he has a soul above appearances."

"You're not his wife," replied the lady who was.

"You may thank your stars!" shouted her too familiar friend.

Little Mrs. Holland turned to her sister and speculated aloud as to the state of the game, but her tone was an example to the ladies in front, who nevertheless did not lower theirs to supply the gratuitous information that the Mundham players had been fielding all day.

"They're getting the worst of it," declared Mrs. Willoughby, perhaps prematurely.

"Do them good," her friend said viciously, but with the soft pedal down for once. "There would have been no holding them. That young Dromard, now—it will take it out of *him*. He wants it taking out of him!"

Mr. Stanley Dromard, who had been scoring heavily all the week, happened to be in the deep field close to the tent. Ruth nudged her sister, and they moved further along their row in order to avoid the bonnets in front.

"Horrid people!" whispered Ruth.

"That's the earl by the canvas screen," answered Tiny. "I should like to send him a new straw hat!"

"Hush!" whispered Ruth in terror. "You're as bad as they are. Tell me, do you see Herbert?"

"Yes, there he is, all by himself. There's a man out."

"Is there? How tired they seem! That's Lord Manister sprawling on the grass. What a boy he looks! You wouldn't think he was anybody in particular, would you?"

"I should hope not, indeed, on the cricket field!"

"I only meant he looked rather nice."

"Certainly he looks nicer in flannels than in anything else; his tailor has less to do with it."

The patience of Ruth was inexhaustible. She watched the game until another wicket fell. Then it was her admiration for the scene that escaped in more whispers.

"*Isn't* it a lovely place, Tiny?"

"Oh, it's all that."

"I've never seen one to touch it, and I have seen two or three, you know, since we were married. But the house is the best part of it all. I would give anything to live in a house like that—wouldn't you?"

"I? My immortal soul!"

And Tiny sighed, but Ruth, looking round quickly, saw laughter in her eyes, and said no more. Tiny was very trying. Was she half in earnest, or wholly in jest? Ruth could never tell; and now, while she wondered, a lady who knew her sat down on her right. Ruth was glad enough to shake hands and talk, and not sorry in this case to be seen doing so, while at the moment it was a very human pleasure to her to leave Tiny to take care of herself. And that was a thing at which Tiny may be said to have excelled, so far as one saw, and no further. The attacks of most tongues she was capable of repelling with distinction; against those of her own thoughts she made ever the feeblest resistance; and at this stage of Christina's career her own thoughts were a swarm of flies upon a wound in her heart. That was the truth—and no one suspected it.

During the next quarter of an hour the innings came to an end, and the fielders trooped over to the group of tents at another side of the ground. Tiny hoped that one of them would have the good taste to come to the ladies' tent and talk to her; an Eton boy would do very well; Herbert would be better than nobody: but she hoped in vain. On her right Ruth had turned her back, and was quite taken up with the lady with whom she was not sorry to be seen in conversation. The chairs on her left were all empty; and those flies were fighting for her heart. It was the rustle of silk disturbed them in the end; and Lady Dromard who sat down in the empty chair on Tiny's left.

"I am so glad to see you both," said the countess as though she meant it; and she leant over to shake hands with Ruth, whose back was now turned upon her new found friend. Not so much was said to the pair in front, though those ladies had something to say for themselves. Lady Dromard gave them very small change in smiles, but made the conversation general for a minute or two, with that graceful tact at which, perhaps, she was, in a manner, a professional. With equal facility she dropped them from her talk one after another, much as the last wickets had fallen in the match, and until only Tiny was left in. For the countess had come there expressly to talk to Miss Luttrell, as she herself stated with charming directness.

"I was afraid you were feeling dull; though really you deserve to, Miss Luttrell."

"I was," said Tiny honestly; "but I don't know what I have done to deserve to, Lady Dromard."

"It's the last match, and a poor one, which nobody cares anything about. You should have come earlier in the week."

"We were here on Wednesday afternoon."

"But why not oftener? My second son made ninety-three on Thursday. I do wish you had seen that!"

"It wasn't my fault that I didn't," remarked Miss Luttrell. "I suppose things came in the way."

"Then you are a cricketer!" exclaimed the countess. "I am glad to hear it, for I am a great cricketer myself. No, I don't play, Miss Luttrell; only I know all about it."

Christina candidly confessed that she was not a cricketer in any sense—that, in fact, she knew very little about cricket; and the countess, who considered how many girls would have pretended to know much, was more pleased with this answer than she would have been with an exhibition of real knowledge of the game.

"My only interest in this match, however," explained Lady Dromard, "is in my eldest son. I do so want him to make runs! He has been dreadfully unsuccessful all the week."

Christina was discreetly sympathetic.

"He is going in first," murmured the countess presently in suppressed excitement. "We must watch the match."

So they sat without speaking during the first few overs, and the silence did much for Christina, by putting her at her ease in the hour when she needed all the ease at her command. Cool as she was outwardly, in her heart she was not a little afraid of Lady Dromard, whose manner toward herself had already struck her as rather too kind and much too scrutinizing. She now entertained a perfectly private conviction that Lady Dromard either knew something about her or had her suspicions. Not that this made Christina particularly uncomfortable at the moment. The countess had eyes and wits for the game only, following it intently through a heavy field glass grown light now that Manister was batting.

It was difficult to realize that this eager, animated woman was the mother of the young fellow at the wicket, she looked so very little older than her son; or so it seemed to Tiny, who now had ample opportunity to study not only her face and figure, but her quiet, handsome bonnet and faultless dress. Even Tiny could not help admiring Lady Dromard. Suddenly, however, the hand that held the field-glass was allowed to drop, and the fine face flushed with disappointment as a round of applause burst from the field and found no echo in the tents.

"Manister is out!" exclaimed the countess. "He has only made two or three!"

"How fond she is of him," thought the girl, still watching her companion's face, which somehow softened Christina toward both mother and son; so that now it was with real sympathy that she remarked, "Poor Lord Manister! I am very sorry."

Some expressions of condolence from the seats in front threw the young girl's words into advantageous relief.

The countess said presently to Christina, "I am sorry it has turned out so dull a day; the ground looks really nice when it is fine and sunny."

"It is a beautiful ground," answered Tiny simply; "the trees are so splendid."

"Ah, but you're used to splendid trees."

"In Australia? Well, we are and we are not, Lady Dromard. I mean to say, there are tremendous trees in some parts; in others there are none at all, you know. Up the bush, where we used to live, the trees were of very little account."

"I thought the bush was nothing *but* trees," remarked Lady Dromard; and Christina could not help smiling as she explained the comprehensive character of "the bush."

"So you were actually brought up on a sheep farm!" said Lady Dromard, looking flatteringly at the graceful young girl.

"Yes—on a station. It was in the bush, and very much the bush," laughed Tiny, "for we were hundreds of miles up country. But most of the trees were no higher than this tent, Lady Dromard. The homestead was in a clump of pines, and they were pretty tall, but the rest were mere scrub."

"Then how in the world," cried her ladyship, "did you manage to become educated? What school could you go to in a place like that?"

"We never went to school at all," Tiny informed her confidentially. "We had a governess."

"Ah, and she taught you to sing! I should like to meet that governess. She must be a very clever person."

Her ladyship's manner was delightfully blunt.

"Now, Lady Dromard, you're laughing at me! I know nothing—I have read nothing."

"I rejoice to hear it!" cried the countess cordially. "I assure you, Miss Luttrell, that's a most refreshing confession in these days. Only it's too good to be true. I don't believe you, you know."

Christina made no great effort to establish the truth of her statement; for some minutes longer they watched the game.

But the countess was not interested, though her younger son had gone in, and had already begun to score. "What were they?" she said at length with extreme obscurity; but Christina was polite enough not to ask her what she meant until she had put this question to herself, and while she still hesitated

Lady Dromard recollected herself, appreciated the hesitation, and explained. "I mean the trees in the bush, at your farm. Were they gum trees?"

"Very few of them—there are hardly any gum trees up there."

"Do you know that *I* have a young gum tree?" said Lady Dromard amusingly, as though it were a young opossum.

"No!" said Tiny incredulously.

"But I have, in the conservatory; you might have seen it the other evening."

"How I wish I had!"

The young girl's face wore a flush of genuine animation. Lady Dromard regarded it for a moment, and admired it very much; then she bent forward and touched Ruth on the arm.

"Mrs. Holland, will you trust your sister to me for half an hour? I want to show her something that will interest her more than the cricket."

"Oh, Lady Dromard, I can't think of taking you away from the match," cried Christina, while Ruth's eyes danced, and the bonnets in front turned round.

"My dear Miss Luttrell, it will interest *me* more, now that Lord Manister is out."

"But there's Mr. Dromard."

"Oh, that boy! He has made more runs this week than are good for him. Miss Luttrell, am I to go alone?"

The bonnets in front knocked together.

CHAPTER XII.
ORDEAL BY BATTLE.

If Tiny Luttrell suffered at all from self-consciousness as she followed Lady Dromard from the tent, she hid it uncommonly well. Her color did not change, while her expression was neither bashful nor bold, and unnatural only in its entire naturalness. Considering that the conversation in the ladies' tent underwent a momentary lull, by no means so slight as to escape a sensitive ear, the girl's serene bearing at the countess' skirts was in its way an achievement of which no one thought more highly than Lady Dromard herself. Christina had not merely imagined that she was being systematically watched. No sooner were they in the open air than the countess wheeled abruptly, expecting to surprise some slight embarrassment, not unpardonable in so young a face; and this was not the only occasion on which she was agreeably disappointed in little Miss Luttrell. The short cut to the house was a narrow path that crossed an intervening paddock. They followed this path. But now Lady Dromard walked behind, with eyes slightly narrowed; and still she approved.

Presently they reached the conservatory. It was large and lofty, and the smooth white flags and spreading fronds gave it an appearance of coolness and quiet very different from Christina's recollection of the place on the night of the dance, when Chinese lanterns had shone and smoked and smelt among the foliage, and a frivolous hum had filled the air. The gum tree proved to be a sapling of no great promise or pretensions. Nor was it seen to advantage, being planted in the central bed, in the midst of some admirable palms and tree-ferns. But Tiny made a long arm to seize the leaves and pull them to her nostrils, setting foot on the soft soil in her excitement; and when she started back, with an apology for the mark, her face was beaming.

"But that was a real whiff of Australia," she added gratefully—"the first I've had since I sailed. It was very, very good of you to bring me, Lady Dromard. If you knew how it reminds me!"

"I thought it would interest you," remarked Lady Dromard, who was herself more interested in the footprint on the soil, which was absurdly small. "If you like I will show you something that should remind you still more."

"Oh, of course I like to see anything Australian; but I am sure I am troubling you a great deal, Lady Dromard!"

"Not in the least, my dear Miss Luttrell. I have something extremely Australian to show you now."

Countess Dromard led the way through the room in which Tiny had danced. It was still carpetless and empty, and the clatter of her walking shoes on the floor which her ball slippers had skimmed so noiselessly struck a note that jarred. The desire came over Tiny to turn back. As they passed through the hall, a side door stood open; the girl saw it with a gasp for the open air. It was an odd sensation, as of the march into prison. It made her lag while it lasted; when it passed it was as though weights had been removed from her feet. She ran lightly up the shallow stairs; Lady Dromard was waiting on the landing, and led her along a corridor.

Here Tiny forgot that her feet had drummed vague misgivings into her mind; she could no longer hear her own steps the corridor was so thickly carpeted. It was a special corridor, leading to a very special room of delicate tints and dainty furniture, and Christina was so far herself again as to enter without a qualm. But her qualms had been a rather singular thing.

"This is my own little chapel of ease, Miss Luttrell," the countess explained; "and now do you not see a fellow-countryman?"

She pointed to the window; and in front of the window was a pedestal supporting a gilded cage, and in the cage a pink-and-gray parrot, of a kind with which the girl had been familiar from her infancy. "Oh, you beauty!" cried Christina, going to the cage and scratching the bird's head through the wires. "It's a galar," she added.

"Indeed," said Lady Dromard, watching her; "a galar! I must remember that. By the way, can you tell me why he doesn't talk?"

Christina answered, in a slightly preoccupied manner, that galars very seldom did. She had become quite absorbed in the bird; she seemed easily pleased. She went the length of asking whether she might take him out, and received a hesitating permission to do so at her own risk, Lady Dromard confessing that for her own part she was quite afraid to touch him through the wires. In a twinkling the girl had the bird in her hand, and was smoothing its feathers with her chin. The sun was beginning to struggle through the clouds; the window faced the west; and the faint rays, falling on the young girl's face and the bird's bright plumage, threw a good light on a charming picture. Lady Dromard was reminded of the artificial art of her young days, when this was a favorite posture, and searched narrowly for artifice in her guest. Finding none she admired more keenly than before, but became also more timid on the other's account, so that she could fancy the blood sliding down the fair skin which the beak actually touched.

"Dear Miss Luttrell, do put him back! I tremble for you."

Tiny put the quiet thing back on the perch. Then she turned to Lady Dromard with rather a comic expression.

"Do you know what we used to do with this gentleman up on the station?" said Tiny shamefacedly. "We poisoned him wholesale to save our crop. But this one seems like an old friend to me. Lady Dromard, you have taken me back to the bush this afternoon!"

"So it appears," observed the countess dryly, "or I think you would admire my little view. That's Gallow Hill, and I'm rather proud of my view of it, because it is the only hill of any sort in these parts. Then the sun sets behind it, and those three trees stand out so."

"Ah! I have often wanted to climb up to those three trees," said Tiny, who took a tantalized interest in Gallow Hill; "but I mayn't, because I'm in England, where trespassers will be prosecuted."

For a moment Lady Dromard stared. Then she saw that Christina had merely forgotten. "Dear me, that stupid notice board!" exclaimed the countess. "Lord Dromard never meant it to apply to everybody. Next time you come here come over Gallow Hill, and through the little green gate you can just see. You will find it a quarter of the distance."

Christina had indeed spoken without thinking of Gallow Hill as a part of the estate, or of the warning to trespassers as Lord Dromard's doing. Now she apologized, and was naturally a little confused; but this time the countess would not have had her otherwise. "You shall go back that way this very evening," she said kindly, "and I promise you shan't be prosecuted." But Christina had to pet her fellow-countryman for a minute or two before she quite regained her ease, while her ladyship touched the bell and ordered tea.

"How fond you must be of the bush!" Lady Dromard exclaimed as the girl still lingered by the cage.

"I like it very much," said Christina soberly.

"Better than Melbourne?"

"Oh, infinitely."

"And England?"

"Yes, better than England—I can't help it," Tiny added apologetically.

"There's no reason why you should," said Lady Dromard, with a smile. "I could imagine your quite disliking England after Australia. I'm sure my son disliked it when he first came back."

"Did he?" the girl said indifferently. "Ah, well! I don't dislike England. I admire it very much, and, of course, it is ever so much better than Australia in every way. We have no villages like Essingham out there, no red tiles and old churches, and certainly no villagers who treat you like a queen on wheels when you walk down the street. We've nothing of that sort—nor of this sort either—no splendid old houses and beautiful old grounds! But I can't help it, I'd rather live out there. Give me the bush!"

"You *are* enthusiastic about the bush," said Lady Dromard, laughing; "yet you don't know how fresh enthusiasm is to one nowadays."

"I'm afraid I'm not enthusiastic about anything else, then," answered Christina with engaging candor. "They tell me I don't half appreciate England; I disappoint all my friends here."

"Ah, that is perhaps your little joke at our expense!"

Christina was on the brink of an audacious reply when a footman entered with the tea tray. That took some of the audacity out of her. She had not heard the order given. Once more she reflected where she was, and with whom, and once more she wished herself elsewhere. It was a mild return of her panic downstairs. Now she felt vaguely apprehensive and as vaguely exultant. In the uncertain fusion of her feelings she was apt to become a little unguarded in what she said; there was safety in her sense of this tendency, however.

Lady Dromard was reflecting also. As the footman withdrew she had told him not to shut the door. The truth was she had got Christina to herself by pure design, though she had not originally intended to get her to herself up here. That had been an inspiration of the moment, and even now Lady Dromard was by no means sure of its wisdom. She had gone so far as to closet herself with this girl, but she did not wish the proceeding to appear so pronounced either to the footman or to the girl herself. It would make the footman talk, while it might frighten the girl. That, at any rate, was the idea of Countess Dromard, who, however, had not yet learnt her way about the young mind with which she was dealing.

The tea tray had been placed on a small table near the window. Lady Dromard promptly settled herself with her back to the light, and motioned Christina to a chair facing her.

"Now you'll be able to watch your beloved bird," said her ladyship craftily. "I thought we might as well have tea now we are here. I thought it would be so much more comfortable than having it in the tent."

Tiny settled a business matter by stating that she took two pieces of sugar, but only one spot of cream. Unconsciously, however, she had followed Lady Dromard's advice, for her eyes were fixed on the parrot in the cage.

"I have only had him a few months," observed the countess suggestively. "Something less than a year, I should say."

"Yes?" And Tiny lowered her eyes politely to her hostess' face.

"Yes," repeated Lady Dromard affirmatively. "My son brought him home for me. It was the only present he had time to get, so I rather value it."

The girl's gaze returned involuntarily to the bird she had caressed; apparently her interest was neither diminished nor increased by this information as to its origin.

"He was in a great hurry to run away from us, was he not?" she remarked inoffensively; but there was no attempt in her manner to conceal the fact that Christina knew what she was talking about.

"He was obliged to return rather suddenly," said the countess after a moment's hesitation. She made a longer pause before slyly adding, "I consider myself very lucky to have got him back at all."

"How is that, Lady Dromard?"

And Christina outstared the countess, so that she was asked whether she would not take another cup of tea. She would, and her hand neither rattled it empty nor spilt it full. Then Lady Dromard smiled at the coronet on her teaspoon, and said to it:

"The fact is I was terrified lest he should go and marry one of you."

"One of *us*?"

"Some fascinating Australian beauty," said Lady Dromard hastily. "So many aids-de-camp have done that."

"Poor—young—men!" said Tiny, as slowly and solemnly as though her words were going to the young men's funeral. "It would have been a calamity indeed."

So far from showing indignation Lady Dromard leant forward in her chair to say in her most winning manner:

"I should have been all the more terrified had I known *you*, Miss Luttrell!"

Clearly this was meant for one of those blunt effective compliments to which Lady Dromard had the peculiar knack of imparting delicacy and grace. But the words were no sooner uttered than she saw their double meaning, and grimly awaited the obvious misconstruction. Tiny, however, had a quick perception, and plenty of common sense in little things. Instead of a snub the countess received a good-tempered smile, for which she could not help feeling grateful at the time; but now her instinct told her that she was dealing with a person with whom it might be well to be a little more downright, and she obeyed her instinct without further delay.

"Miss Luttrell, I am sure there is no occasion for me to beat about the bush—with you," she began in an altered, but a no less flattering tone; "I see that one is quite safe in being frank with you. The fact is—and you know it—my son very nearly did marry someone out there. Now you met him out there in society, and you probably knew everyone there who was worth knowing, so pray don't pretend that you know nothing about this."

Their eyes were joined, but at the moment Christina's was the cooler glance.

"I couldn't pretend that, Lady Dromard, for it happens that I know *all* about it."

The countess was perceptibly startled. "The girl was a friend of yours?" she inquired quickly.

"A great friend," answered Tiny, nodding.

"How I wish you would tell me her name!"

"I mustn't do that." This was said decidedly. "But it seems a strange thing that you don't know it."

"It is a strange thing," Lady Dromard allowed; "nevertheless it's the truth. I never heard her name. You may imagine my curiosity. Miss Luttrell, I seem to have felt ever since I met you that you knew something about this—that you could tell one something. And I don't mind confessing to you now—since I see you are not the one to misunderstand me willfully—that I have purposely sought an opportunity of sounding you on the subject."

Christina smiled, for this was not news to her.

"My son will tell me nothing," continued Lady Dromard, "and I have, of course, the greatest curiosity to know everything. It is no idle curiosity, Miss Luttrell. I am his mother, and he has never got over that attachment."

"Has he not?" said Tiny with dry satire.

"He has never got over it," repeated Lady Dromard in a tone which was a match for the other. "Has the girl?"

Tiny was startled in her turn. She hesitated before replying, and seemed to waver over the nature of her reply. It was the first sign she had shown of wavering at all, and Lady Dromard drew her breath. The girl was hanging her head, and murmuring that she really could not answer for the other girl. Suddenly she flung up her face, and it was hot, but not hotter than her words:

"Yes, Lady Dromard, you are his mother. But the girl was my friend. He treated her abominably!"

"It wasn't his fault—it was mine," said Lady Dromard steadily.

"I'm afraid that does not make one think any better of him," murmured the young girl. Her chin was resting in her hand. The flush had passed from her face as suddenly as it had come. Her eyes were raised to the sky out of the window, and there was in them the sad, hardened, reckless look that those who knew her best had seen too often, latterly, in her silent moments. The sun was dropping clear of the clouds, and the brighter rays fell kindly over Tiny's dark hair and pale, piquant face. The keen eye that was on her had never watched more closely nor admired so much.

"Consider!" said Lady Dromard presently, and rather gently. "Try to put yourself in our place—and consider. We have a position, here in England, of which very few people can be got to take a sensible view; half the country professes an absurd contempt for it, while the other half speaks of it and of us with bated breath. We ourselves naturally think something of our position, and we try, as we say, to keep it up. Of course we are worldly, in the popular sense. We bring up our children with worldly ideas. They must make worldly marriages in their own station. Is it so very contemptible that we should see to this, and dread beyond most things an unwise or an unequal marriage? Now do consider: we let our son go out to Australia, because it is good for a young man to see the world before he marries and settles down—and mind! that was what he was about to do. If he had not gone to Australia then, he would have been married at once. He was all but engaged. It was a case of putting off the engagement instead of the marriage. We do not believe in long, formal engagements; we do not permit them. We find them undesirable for many reasons. So, you see, he goes out to Australia as good as engaged, but unable to say so, and very young, and no doubt very susceptible. Can you wonder that I tremble for him when he has gone? Well, he is the best son in the world, and has told me everything always. That is my comfort. But presently he tells one things in his letters which make one tremble more than ever, though he tells them jokingly. Then a cousin of Lord Dromard's stays a day or two in Melbourne and comes home with a report——"

Christina's face twitched in the sunlight. "I suppose that was Captain Dromard?" she said quietly; "I never met him, but I saw him." She seemed to see him then, and that was why her face twitched. She was still staring out of the window at the yellowing sky.

"Captain Dromard had forgotten the girl's name," said the countess pointedly; "but he told me enough to make me write to my boy—I nearly cabled! And do you think I was wrong?"

"Not from your point of view, Lady Dromard," answered Christina judicially, with her eyes half closed in the slanting sunbeams which she chose to face. "Certainly you cannot have had very much faith in Lord Manister's judgment; but the case is altered if he was to all intents and purposes engaged to a girl in England; and, at all events, that's the worst that could be said of you—looking at it from your own point of view. But is not the girl out there entitled to a point of view as well?" And the hardened reckless eyes were turned so suddenly upon Lady Dromard that the youth and grace and bitterness of the girl smote her straight to the heart.

There was a slight tremor and great tenderness in the voice that whispered, "Did she feel it very much? Come, come—don't tell me it broke her heart!"

"No, I won't tell you that," said the girl briskly, but with a laugh which hurt. "That doesn't break so easily in these days. No, it didn't break her heart, Lady Dromard—it did much worse. It got her talked about. It poisoned her mind, it killed her faith, it spoilt her temper. It did all that—and one thing worse still. Though it didn't *break* her heart, Lady Dromard, it cracked it, so that it will never ring true any more; it made her hate those she had loved—those who loved her; it made it impossible for her ever to care for anybody in the whole wide world again!"

Lady Dromard had drawn her chair nearer to the girl, and nearer still. Lady Dromard was no longer mistress of herself.

"Did it make her hate *you*, my dear?"

"It made her loathe—me."

Lady Dromard was seen to battle with a strong womanly impulse, and to lose. Her fine eyes filled with tears. Her soft, white hands flew out to Christina's, and drew them to her bosom. At this moment a young man in flannels appeared at the door, and the young man was Lord Manister; but the rich carpet had muffled his tread, and the two women had eyes for one another only—the girl he had loved—the mother who had drawn him from her. The same sunbeam washed them both.

"Now I know her name—now I know it!"

"I think you cannot have found it out this minute, Lady Dromard."

"But I have. I have never known whether to believe it or not, since it first crossed my mind, the night you dined here. You see, I know him so well! But he didn't tell me, and after all I had no reason to suppose it. Oh, he has told me nothing—and you are the gulf between us, for which I have only myself to thank. Ah, if I had only dreamt—of you!"

Tiny suffered herself to be kissed upon the cheek.

"Pray say no more, dear Lady Dromard," she said quietly. "Shall I tell you why?" she added, drawing back. "Why, because it's quite a thing of the past."

"It is not a thing of the past," cried Lady Dromard passionately. "He has never loved anyone else. He bitterly regrets having listened to me, and I, now that I know you—I bitterly regret everything! And he loves you ... and I would rather ... and I have told him what is the simple truth—how I have admired you from the first!"

The last sentence was doubtless a mistake. It was the only one that would let itself be uttered, however, and before another could be added by either woman Lord Manister had tramped into the room. They fell the further apart as he came between them and stooped down, laying his hands heavily on the little table. His eyes sped from the girl to his mother, and back to the girl, on whom they stayed. One hand held his crumpled cap. His hair was disordered. In many ways he looked at his best, as Tiny had always said he did in flannels. But never before had Tiny seen him half so earnest and sad and handsome.

"My mother is right," he said firmly. "I love you, and I ask you to forgive us both, and to give me what I don't deserve—one word of hope!"

The young girl glanced from his grave, humble face to that of his mother, through whose tears a smile was breaking. Lady Dromard's lips were parted, half in surprise at the humility of her son's words, half in eagerness for the answer to them. Tiny Luttrell read her like a printed book, and rose to her feet with a smile that was equally unmistakable, for it was a smile of triumph.

CHAPTER XIII.
HER HOUR OF TRIUMPH.

Now Herbert was taking part in the match, and Ruth was in the ladies' tent, trying not to think of Christina, who was playing a single-wicket game in another place. But Erskine Holland was rolling the rectory court gloomily and quite alone, and he was tired of Essingham. Not only had the day kept fine in spite of its threats, but toward the end of the afternoon it turned out very fine indeed, and the light became excellent for lawn tennis, because there was nobody to play with poor Erskine. Even the good Willoughby was on the accursed field over yonder; and he mattered least. Ruth was there. Tiny was there. Herbert was not only there, but playing for Lord Manister, who was notoriously short of men. One can hardly wonder at Erskine's condemnation of his brother-in-law, out of his own mouth, as a stultified young fraud in the matter of Lord Manister. As to the girls, some old tenets of his concerning women in general returned to taunt him for the ship-wreck of his holiday at least. Yet Ruth had but plotted for her sister's advancement, not her own. Whether Christina cared in the least for the man whom she evidently meant to marry, if she could, was, after all, Christina's own affair. Erskine had only heard her disparage him behind his back—at which Herbert himself could not beat her—whereas Ruth had at least been openly in favor of the fellow from the very first. But if Herbert was a fraud, what was the name for Tiny? Clearly the only trustworthy person of the three was Ruth, who at least—yet alone—was consistent.

To this conclusion, which was not without its pleasing side, Erskine came with his eyes on the ground he was rolling. But as he pushed the roller toward the low stone wall dividing the lawn from the churchyard, into which the balls were too often hit, one came whizzing out of it for a change, and struck the roller under Erskine's nose. And leaning with her elbows on the low wall, and her right hand under her chin, as though it were the last right hand that could have flung that ball, stood the girl for whom a bad enough name had yet to be found.

"Where on earth did you spring from?" Holland asked, a little brusquely, as he stopped for a moment and then rolled on toward the wall.

"If you mean the ball," replied Tiny, "it must be the one we lost the last time we played. I have just found it among the graves, and it slipped out of my hand."

"I meant you," said Erskine, with an unsuccessful smile; and he pushed the roller close up to the wall, and folded his arms upon the handle.

"Oh, I have come from the hall by the forbidden path over Gallow Hill; but it seems that wasn't meant for us, and at any rate I have leave to use it whenever I like." She was puzzling him, and she knew it, but she met his eyes with a mysterious smile for some moments before adding: "You can't think what a view there is from the top of the hill—I mean a view of the hall. Just now the sun was blazing in all the windows, like the flash of a broadside from an old two-decker; you see it made such an impression on me that I thought of that for your benefit."

Erskine acknowledged the benefit rather heavily with a nod.

"What have you done with Ruth?"

"To the best of my belief she is watching the match; at least she was an hour ago."

"Something *has* happened!" exclaimed Erskine Holland, starting upright and leaving the roller handle swinging in the air like an inverted pendulum. His eyes were unconsciously stern; those of the girl seemed to quail before them.

"Something has happened," she admitted to the top of the wall. "I suppose you would get to know sooner or later, so I may as well tell you myself now. The fact is Lord Manister has just proposed to me."

Erskine dropped his eyes and shrugged slightly; then he raised them to the setting sun, and tried to look resigned; then, with a noticeable effort, he brought them back to her face, and forced a smile.

"I'm not surprised. I saw it coming, though I hardly expected it so soon. Well, Tiny, I congratulate you! He is about the most brilliant match in England."

"Quite the most, I thought?"

"And I am sure he is a first-rate fellow," added Erskine with vigor, regretting that he had not said this first, and disliking what he had said.

"Oh, he is a very good sort," acknowledged Tiny to the wall.

"So you ought to be the happiest young woman in the world, as you are perhaps the luckiest—I mean in one sense. And I congratulate you, Tiny, I do indeed!"

To clinch his congratulations he held out his hand, from which she raised her eyes to him at last—with the look of a cabman refusing his proper fare.

"And I took you for the most discerning person I knew!" said Tiny very slowly.

"You don't mean to say——"

His eagerness and incredulity arrested his speech.

"I *do* mean to say."

"That you have—refused him?"

Tiny nodded. "With thanks—not too many."

They stared at one another for some moments longer. Then Erskine sat down on the roller and folded his arms and looked extremely serious, though already the corners of his mouth were beginning to twitch.

"Now, you know, Tiny, I'm *in loco parentis* as long as you're in England. In this one matter you've no business to chaff me. Honestly, now, is it the truth that Lord Manister has asked you to marry him, and that you have said him nay?"

"It is the truest truth I ever uttered in my life. I refused him point-blank," added Tiny, with eyes once more lowered, as though the memory were not unmixed with shame, "and before his own mother!"

"In the presence of Lady Dromard?"

She nodded solemnly, but with a blush.

"Good Lord!" murmured Erskine. "And I was ass enough to think you were leading him on!"

She whispered, "And so I was."

For one moment Erskine stared at her more seriously than ever; then the reaction came, and she saw him shaking. He shook until the tears were in his eyes; and when he was rid of them he perceived the same thing in Tiny's eyes, but obviously not from the same cause.

"*I* don't think it's such a joke," said the girl, in the voice of one pained when in pain already. "I am pretty well ashamed of myself, I can tell you. If you really consider yourself responsible for me I think you might let me tell you something about it; for you must tell Ruth—I daren't. But if you're going to laugh ... let me tell you it's no laughing matter to me, now I've done it."

"Forgive me," said Holland instantly; "I am a brute. Do tell me anything you care to; I promise not to laugh unless you do. And I might be able to help you."

"Ah, you would if anybody could; but nobody can; I have behaved just scandalously, and I know it as well as you do, now that it's too late. Yet I wish that you knew all about it, Erskine!" She looked at him wistfully. "You understand things so. Would it bore you if I were to tell you how the whole thing happened?"

The gilt hands of the church clock made it ten minutes to six when Erskine shook his head and bent it attentively. When the hour struck he had opened his mouth only once, to answer her question as to how much he knew of her affair with Lord Manister in Melbourne. He had known for a day and a half as much as Ruth knew; and he did not learn much more now, for the girl could speak more freely of recent incidents, and dwelt principally on those of that afternoon, beginning with Lady Dromard's extraordinary attentiveness on the cricket field.

"I felt there was something behind that, though I didn't know what; I could only be sure that she had her eye on me. However, I took a tremendous vow to face whatever came without moving a muscle. I think I succeeded, on the whole, but I was on the edge of a panic when she took me upstairs. I wanted to clear! I had qualms!"

She was startlingly candid on another point.

"I also made up my mind to behave as prettily as possible, just to show her. I was really pleased with the interest she seemed to take in what I told her about the bush, and I was quite delighted to see a galar again. But I needn't have made the fuss I did in taking it out of its cage; that was purely put on, and all the time I was mortally afraid that it would peck me. Yet I suppose," added Tiny, after some moments, "you won't believe me when I tell you that I am ashamed of all that already?"

Erskine declared that there was nothing in the world to be ashamed of; on the contrary, in his opinion she was perfectly justified in all she had done. With kind eyes upon her, he added what he very nearly meant, that he was proud of her; and his remark wrought a change in her expression which convinced him finally that at least she was not proud of herself.

"Ah, you weren't there, Erskine," said Christina sadly, her blue eyes clouded with penitence; "you don't know how kind poor Lady Dromard was with all her dodges! She said it would be more comfortable to have tea up there. Comfortable was the last thing I felt in my heart, but I never let her see that; and besides, I didn't as yet guess what was coming. Even when she wanted me to tell her my own name, I couldn't be sure that she suspected me. I wasn't sure until she asked me whether the girl had got over it, when I knew from her voice. And I saw then that she really rather liked me, and half wished it to be; and I was sorry because I liked her; and though I spoke my mind to her about her son, I should have made a clean breast of everything to her if he hadn't come in just then. I should have told her straight that I didn't care *that* for him—not now—and that I had been flirting with him disgracefully just to try to make him smart as I had smarted. That's the whole truth of it, Erskine; and I meant to tell her so in another second, because I couldn't stand her kissing me and crying, and all that. I should have been crying myself next moment. But just then *he* came in, and I remembered everything. I remembered, too, what she had had to do with it, on her own showing; and when I saw what she wanted me to say I think I became possessed."

Her brother-in-law was very curious to know all that Christina had said, but she would not tell him. She merely remarked that he would think all the worse of her if he knew, even though at the moment she could hardly remember any one thing that she had said. Then she paused, and recalled a little, and the little made her blush.

"I didn't come well out of it," she declared.

Erskine threw discredit on her word in this particular matter; he sniffed an extravagant remorse.

"Talk of hitting a man when he's down!" exclaimed Tiny miserably. "I hit Lady Dromard when the tears were in her eyes, and Lord Manister when he was hitting himself. He took it splendidly. He is a gentleman. I don't care what else he is—lord or no lord, he would always be a perfect gentleman. What's more, I am very sorry for him."

"Why on earth be sorry for him?" asked Erskine with a touch of irritation; for when Tiny spoke of Lady Dromard's tears, her own eyes swam with them; and to do a thing like this and start crying over it the moment it was done seemed to Erskine a bad sign. The event was so very fresh, and so entirely contrary to his own most recent apprehensions, that at present his only feeling in the matter was one of profound satisfaction. But the symptoms she showed of relenting already interfered not a little with that satisfaction, while, even more than by the remark that had prompted his question, he was alarmed by her answer to it:

"Because I believe he does care for me, a little bit, in his own way—or he thinks he does, which comes to the same thing; and because, when all's said and done, I have treated him like a little fiend!"

"My good girl!" said Holland uneasily, "I should remember how he treated you."

"Ah, no," answered Christina, shaking her head; "I have remembered that far too long as it is. That's ancient history."

"Well, be sorry for him if you like; be sorry for yourself as well."

That was the best advice that occurred to him at the moment, but it set her off at a tangent.

"I should think I am sorry for myself—I should be sorry for any girl who could so far forget herself!" cried Christina, speaking bitterly and at a great pace. "Shall I tell you the sort of thing I said? When I told him I could not possibly believe in his really caring for me, after the way in which he left

Melbourne without so much as saying good-by to me or sending me word that he was going, he said it wasn't then he really loved me, but now. So I told him I was sorry to hear it, as in my case it might perhaps have been then, but it certainly wasn't now. I actually said that! Then Lady Dromard spoke up. She had been staring at me without a word, but she spoke up now, and it served me right. I can't blame her for being indignant, but she didn't say half she could have said, and it was more what she implied that sticks and stings. It didn't sting then, though; I was thinking of all the talk out there. It was when Lord Manister stopped her, and held out his hand to me and said, 'Anyway you forgive me now? I thought you *had* forgiven me'—it was then I began to tingle. I said I forgave him, of course; and then I bolted. But I was sorry for him, and I *am* sorry for him, whatever you say, for I had cut him to the heart.... And he looked most awfully nice the whole time!"

With these frivolous last words there came a smile: the normal girl shone out for an instant, as the sun breaks through clouds; and Erskine took advantage of the gleam.

"To the heart of his vanity—that's where you cut. You've humiliated him certainly; but surely he deserved it? In any case, you've given young Manister the right-about; and upon my soul that's rather a performance for our Tiny! I should only like to have seen it."

"It's good of you to call me your Tiny," returned the young girl rather coldly. "But don't talk to me about performances, please, unless you mean disgraceful performances. I wish I had never come to England—I wish I was back in Australia—I wish I was up at the station!" she cried with sudden passion. "I am miserable, and you won't understand me; and Ruth couldn't if she tried."

"My dear girl," Erskine said in rather an injured tone, "surely you're a little unfair on us both? Ruth will understand when I tell her; and as for me—I think I understand you already."

"Not you!" answered Tiny disdainfully. "You call it a performance! You treat it as a joke!" And she left him, with the tears in her eyes.

He watched her enter the garden by the little gate lower down, and saunter toward the house with lagging steps. The low sun streamed upon her drooping figure. Even at that distance, and with her face hidden from him, she seemed to Erskine the incarnation of all that was wayward and willful and sweet in girlhood. And her tears and temper made her doubly sweet, as the rain draws new fragrance from a flower; but they had also made her doubly difficult to understand. One moment he had seen her plainly, as in the lime light; in another, she had retired to a deeper shade than before. The explanation of her conduct toward Lord Manister had been a sufficiently startling revelation, yet a perfectly lucid one; but what of this prompt transition to tears and penitence? The only interpretation which suggested itself to Erskine was one that he refused to entertain. He preferred to attribute Christina's present state of mind to mere reaction; if the reaction had taken a rather hysterical form, that, perhaps, was not to be wondered at. Moreover, this seemed to be indeed the case; for the girl was seen no more that day, save by Ruth, who by night was perhaps the most disappointed person in the parish; only she managed to conceal her disappointment in a way that it was impossible not to admire.

Nevertheless dinner at the rectory was a dismal meal, and the more so for the high spirits of Herbert, which, meeting with no response, turned to silence. Poor Herbert happened to have distinguished himself in the match, which, indeed, he had been largely instrumental in winning for his side; but neither Ruth nor her husband showed any interest in his exploit, and Tiny was not there. Erskine was no cricketer; Herbert hated him for it, and made a sullen attack on the claret. But at length it dawned upon him that there was some special reason for the silence and glum looks at either end of the table, for which Christina's alleged headache would not in itself account; and when Ruth left the table early to look after Tiny, he said bluntly to Erskine:

"You're enough to give a fellow the blues, the pair of you! What's wrong? Have I done anything, or has Tiny?"

Erskine temporized, pushing forward the claret. "I understand *you* have done something," he said with a first approach to geniality; "but, upon my word, old fellow, I don't know what it is. I couldn't listen, for the life of me; and you must forgive me. Tiny's upset, and that's upset Ruth, which I suppose has upset me in my turn. Please call me names—I deserve them—and then tell me again what you have done."

Herbert did not require two invitations to do this. He had not only acquitted himself brilliantly, but there was a peculiar piquancy in his success; he had saved the side which had treated him with unobtrusive but galling contempt until the last moment, when he opened their eyes, and their throats too. They had put him to field at short leg; during the intervals, after the fall of a wicket, not one of them had spoken a word to him, save good-natured Mr. Willoughby; and they had sent him in last, with hopeless faces, when there were many runs to get. The good batsmen, beginning with Lord Manister, had mostly failed miserably. The Honorable Stanley Dromard, who had been in fine form all the week, had alone done well; and he was still at the wicket when Herbert whipped in, with his ears full of gratuitous instructions to keep his wicket up, and not to try to hit the professional, and his heart full of other designs. Those instructions were given without much knowledge of this young Australian, who took a sincere delight in disregarding them. He had hit out from the very first, particularly at the professional, who disliked being hit, and who was also somewhat demoralized by the extreme respect with which he had been treated by preceding batsmen. There were thirty runs to make when Herbert went in, and in a quarter of an hour he made them nearly all from his own bat, exhibiting an almost insolent amount of coolness and nerve at the crisis. The best of it was that no one had considered it a crisis when he went in; but his truculent batting had immediately made it one, and ultimately, in a scene of the greatest excitement, of which Herbert was the hero, an almost certain defeat had been converted into a glorious victory. All this was confirmed by the local newspaper next day; considering his achievement and his character, the hero himself told his tale with modesty.

"He bowled like beggary," he concluded, in allusion to the discomfited professional; "but I tell you, old toucher, we were too many measles for him!"

"They were more civil to you after that?"

"My oath!" said Herbert complacently. "Those Eton jokers kicked up hell's delight! Stanley Dromard shook hands with me between the wickets, and said I ought to be going up to Trinity; but he's a real good sportsman, with less side than you'd think. His governor, the earl, congratulated me in person—you bet I felt it down my marrow! He wants to know how it is I'm not playing for the Australians. The only man who didn't say a word to me was that dam' fool Manister."

"Ah, he was on the ground, then?"

"He turned up as I went in; and when I came out he didn't look at me. Who the blazes does he think he is? I'm as good a man as him, though I'm a larrikin and he's a twopenny lord. I don't care what he is, I had the bulge over him to-day—he made four!"

"Perhaps someone else has had the bulge over him, too," suggested Erskine gently.

"Has someone?"

Erskine nodded.

"Our Tiny?"

"Yes; he has asked her to marry him, and she has refused him on the spot."

Herbert shot out of his chair.

"So're you crackin'! I thought something was *wrong*, man? O Lord, this is a treat!"

"It's a treat she didn't prepare one for. I had visions of a very different upshot."

"Aha! you never know where you have our Tiny. No more does old Manister. Oh, but this is a treat for the gods!"

"I told Tiny it was a performance," Erskine said reflectively; "it struck me as one, and I was trying to cheer her up—but that wasn't the way."

"No? She's a terror, our Tiny!" murmured Herbert, with a running chuckle. "Now I know why the brute was so civil to me the first time I met him in these parts. Even then my hand itched to fill his eye for him, but I didn't say anything, because Tiny seemed on the job herself. To think this was her game! I must go and shake hands with her. I must go and tell her she's done better than filling up his eye."

"Don't you," said Erskine quietly. "I wouldn't say much to her afterward, either, if I may give you a hint. She doesn't take quite our view of this matter. Not that we can pretend that ours is at all a nice view of it, mind you; only I really do regard it as a bit of a performance on our Tiny's part, and I should like to have seen it."

"By ghost, so should I! And seriously," added Herbert, "he deserved all he's got. I happen to know."

CHAPTER XIV.
A CYCLE OF MOODS.

But the girl herself chose to think otherwise. That was her perversity. She could now see excuses for her own ill-treatment in the past, but none for the revenge she had just taken on the man who had treated her badly. A revenge it had certainly been, plotted systematically, and carried out from first to last in sufficiently cold blood. But already she was ashamed of it. So sincerely ashamed was Christina, now that she had completed her retaliation and secured her triumph, that she very much exaggerated the evil she had done, and could imagine no baser behavior than her own. She had, indeed, felt the baseness of it while yet there was time to draw back, but the memory of her own humiliation had been her goad whenever she hesitated; and then the way had been made irresistibly easy for her. But this was no comfort to her now. Neither was that goad any excuse to her self-accusing mind; for she could feel it no longer, which made her wonder how she had ever felt it at all. Her judgment was obscured by the magnitude of her meanness in her own eyes. The revulsion of feeling was as complete as it was startling and distressing to herself.

In her trouble and excitement that night it became necessary for her to speak to someone, and she spoke with unusual freedom to Ruth, who displayed on this occasion, among others, a really lamentable want of tact. Tiny sought to explain her trouble: it was not that she could possibly care for Lord Manister again, or dream of marrying him under any circumstances (Ruth said nothing to all this), but that she half believed he really cared for her (Ruth was sure of it), in his own way (Ruth seemed to believe in his way); and in any case she was very sorry for him. So was Ruth. In all the circumstances the sorrow of Ruth might well have received a less frank expression than she thought fit to give it.

But it is only fair to say that this did not occur to Ruth. She was in and out of the room until at last Christina was asleep, and dreaming of the hall windows ablaze against the sunset, while again and again in her sleep the warm, broken voice of Lady Dromard turned hard and cold. Ruth watched her affectionately enough as she slept, and consoled herself for her own disappointment by the reflection that at least they understood one another now. Therefore it was a rude shock to her when Christina came down next day and would hardly look at any of them.

Her mood had changed; it was now her worst. She was pale still, but her expression was set, and there was a quarrelsome glitter in her eyes; the fact being that she was a little tired of chastising herself, and exceedingly ready to begin on some second person. So Erskine himself was badly snubbed at his own breakfast table, and when Tiny afterward took herself into the kitchen garden Ruth followed her for an explanation, in the fullness of her confidence that they understood one another at last. No explanation was given, Tiny merely remarking that she was sorry if she had been rude, but that she was in an evil state all through, and unfit for human society. To Ruth, however, this only meant that Tiny was unfit to be alone. So Ruth remained in the kitchen garden too, and was good enough to resume gratuitously her consolations of the night before. But in a very few minutes she returned, complaining, to her husband.

"My dear," said he at once, "you oughtn't to have gone near her. Above all, you shouldn't have broached the subject of her affairs; you should have left that to her. She seems considerably ashamed of herself, and though I must say I think that's absurd, you can't help liking her the better for it. She surprised us all, but she surprised herself too, because she has found that she can't strike a blow without hurting herself at least as badly as anybody else; and that shows the good in her. Personally, I think the blow was justified; but that has nothing to do with it. The point is that if she's mortified about the whole concern, as is obviously the case, it must increase her mortification to know that we know all about it, and that she herself has told us. Which applies more to me than to you. It was natural she should tell you; she only told me because I happened to be the first person she saw, and I can quite understand her hating me by this time for listening. We must ignore the whole matter except when it pleases her to bring it up, and then we must let her make the running."

"I hate people to require so much humoring!" exclaimed Ruth, with some reason.

"Well, I must say I'm glad that *you* don't," her husband said prettily. "As to Tiny, her faults are very sweet, and her moods are really interesting—but I'm thankful they don't run in the family!"

He seemed thankful.

"Yet you're a wonderful man for understanding other people," returned Ruth as prettily; and her eyes were full of admiration.

"Ah, well! Tiny's not like other people. I think she must enjoy startling one. Our best plan is to expect the unexpected of her from this time forth, and to let her be until she comes to herself."

And that came to pass quite in good time. Having effaced herself all the morning and again during the afternoon, and having been grotesquely polite to the others (when it was necessary to speak to them) at midday dinner, Tiny appeared at tea in another frock and flying signals of peace. She seemed anxious to acquiesce with things that were said. So Erskine forced jokes which were sufficiently terrible in themselves, but they served a good purpose very well. Christina recovered her old form, and after tea made a winsome assault upon no less redoubtable a defender of his own inclinations than her brother Herbert. Him she successfully importuned to take her to church in the evening, although not to the church close at hand, where there was never, necessarily, any service in the rector's absence. Tiny, however, had heard from her friends in the village of a gifted young Irishman who wore a stole and held forth extempore in a neighboring parish; they found their way to it across the twilight fields. They did not return till after nine, when Christina seemed much brighter than before. Her brightness, however, was seemingly more grateful to Mr. than to Mrs. Holland, who enticed her brother into the garden after supper, to ask him whether Tiny had not mentioned Lord Manister.

"Why, yes, she did just mention him," said Herbert; "but that's all. I wasn't going to say a word about the joker, and just as we came back to the drive here she got a hold of my arm and thanked me for not having asked her any questions; so I was glad I hadn't. She said she wasn't by any means proud of herself, and that she wanted to forget the whole thing, if we'd only let her. She doesn't want to be bothered about it by anybody. Those were her very words, as we came up the drive. She was jolly enough all the way there, talking mostly about Wallandoon. You'll have noticed how keen she is on the station ever since she went up there with the governor last April; I think the old place was a treat to her after Melbourne, to tell you the truth."

Ruth nodded, as much as to say that she knew. She asked, however, whether Tiny had talked also of Wallandoon on the way home.

"No; she was a bit quiet on the way home. I think the sermon must have made an impression on her, but I didn't hear it myself; I put in a sleep instead. In the hymns, though, she sang out immense—by ghost, as if she meant it! I rather wished I'd heard the sermon," remarked Herbert thoughtfully, "because it seemed to set her thinking. I believe she's given to thinking of those things now and then; I shouldn't be surprised to see her go religious some day, if she don't marry; I'd rather she did, too, than marry a thing like Manister!"

The next day was their last at Essingham, for which not even Ruth could grieve, in view of recent events. The day, however, was its own consolation; it was cold and dull and damp, though not actually wet, so that Erskine, who spent the greater part of the morning in front of a barometer, had hopes of some final sets in the afternoon, when the Willoughbys were coming to say good-by. Nor was he disappointed when the time arrived, though the court was dead and the light bad; his own service was the more telling under these conditions. But to the two girls, who had been brought up to better things, it was a repulsive day from all points of view, and they were very glad to spend the morning in packing up before a hearty fire.

"This is the kind of thing that makes one sigh for Wallandoon," Tiny happened to say once as she stood looking out of the window at gray sky and sullied trees. The thought was spoken just as it came into her head with an imaginary beam of bush sunshine. There was no other thought behind it—no human mote in that sunbeam certainly. But Ruth had raised her head swiftly from the trunk over which she was bending, and she knelt gazing at her sister's back as a dog pricks its ears.

"Why Wallandoon? Why not Melbourne?"

"Because I have had enough of Melbourne," replied Christina quietly, and without turning round.

"I thought you took so kindly to it?"

"Perhaps I did; I have taken kindly to many things that were bad for me in my time. And that's all the more reason why I should hanker after Wallandoon. I only wish we could all go back there to live!"

"Well, I must say I shouldn't care to live there now," remarked Ruth, with a little laugh; "and I don't see how you could like it either, after civilization."

"Ah, that's because you never cared for the station as I did," replied Christina, with her back still turned; "you liked the veranda better than the run, and you hated the dust from the sheep when you were riding. I can smell it now! Just think: they'll be in the middle of shearing by this time. They were going to have thirty-six shearers on the board, and they expected the best clip they've had for years. Can't you hear the blades clicking and the tar boys tearing down the board, and the bales being heaved about at the back of the shed—or see the fleeces thrown out on the table and rolled up and bounced into the bins—and father drafting in a cloud of dust at the yards? Can't I! Many's the time I've brought him a mob of woollies myself. And how good the pannikin of tea was, and the shearer's bun! I can taste 'em now. You never cared for tea in a pannikin. Yet perhaps if you'd ever gone back to see the place since we left it, as I did, you might be as keen on it as I am. I own I wasn't so keen when we lived there. When I went back and saw it the other day, though, I thought it the best place in the world; and you would, too."

"Is Jack Swift managing it now?" Ruth asked indifferently.

"You knew he was."

"Really I'm afraid I don't know much about it; but if you're so fond of the place as all that, Tiny, I should just marry Jack Swift, and live there ever after."

"I suppose you're joking," said the young girl rather scornfully; "but in case you aren't perhaps it will relieve you to hear that, if ever I do marry, I shall marry a man—not a place."

And she turned round and stared hard through another window, which commanded a view of the Mundham gates and grounds; and Ruth made no more jokes; but neither, on the other hand, did Tiny expatiate any further on the attractions of station life at Wallandoon.

The Willoughbys came in the afternoon, when Mrs. Willoughby was severely disappointed, owing to the rudeness of Christina, who had disappeared mysteriously, although she knew that these people were coming. Mrs. Willoughby had seen her last leaving the cricket ground at Mundham under the wing of Lady Dromard—Mrs. Willoughby had looked forward immensely to seeing her again. But Christina had gone out, and none knew whither; the visitor's idea was some private engagement at the hall; and this was not the only idea she expressed, a little too freely for the entire ease of Christina's sister. Happily they were only ideas. Mrs. Willoughby knew nothing.

Tiny, as it turned out later, had spent the whole afternoon in the village, saying good-by to her friends there. Ruth found this rather difficult to believe, as she had heard so little of the friends in question. Nevertheless it was strictly true, and Tiny had taken tea with Mrs. Clapperton, whose tears she had kissed away when they said good-by; but that was only the end of a scene which would have been a revelation to some who prided themselves on knowing their Tiny as well as anyone could know so unaccountable a person. At dinner that evening she seemed chastened and subdued, yet her temper, certainly, had never been sweeter. It was noticeable that, while she had a responsive smile for most things that were said, she made fun of nothing herself; and she was far too fond of making fun of everything. But for two whole days her moods had come and gone like the shadows of the clouds when sun and wind are strong together; and the last of her whims was not the least puzzling at the time. Later Ruth read it to her own extreme satisfaction; but at the time it did seem odd to her that anyone should desire a walk on so chilly and unattractive a night. Yet when they had left the men to themselves this was what Tiny said she would like above all things. And Ruth, who humored her, had her reward.

For she found herself being led through the churchyard; and when she hesitated as they came to the notice to trespassers, Tiny muttered in a dare-devil way:

"Lady Dromard gave me leave to come this way whenever I liked, and I mean to make use of my privilege while I can. I want to see the hall once again—it has a sort of fascination for me!"

More amazed than before, Ruth followed her leader up the western slope of Gallow Hill. The night was so dark that they heard the rustle of the beeches on top before they could discern their branches against the sky; and standing under them presently, panting from their climb, they gazed down upon a double row of warm lights embedded in blackness. These were the hall windows, in even tier, with here and there one missing, like the broken teeth of a comb. Outline the building had none; only the windows were bitten upon a sable canvas in ruddy orange and glimmering yellow, from which there was just enough reflection on the lawn and shrubs to chain them to earth in the mind of one who watched.

"Only the windows," murmured Tiny musingly. "Those windows mean to haunt me for the rest of my time."

"I wish it were moonlight," Ruth said. "I wish we could see everything."

"No, I like it best as it is," remarked Tiny, after further meditation. "It leaves something to your imagination. Those windows are going to leave my imagination uncommonly well off!"

They stood together in silence, and the beeches talked in whispers above them. When Ruth spoke next she whispered too, as though they were just outside those lighted windows:

"Yet you would rather live at Wallandoon than anywhere else on earth!"

Tiny said nothing to that; but after it, at a distance, there came a sigh.

"What's the matter, Ruth?"

"I'd rather not tell you, dear; it might make you angry."

"I think I like being made angry just at present," said Christina, with a little laugh; "but you've spiked my guns by saying that first; you are quite safe, my dear."

"Then I was thinking—I couldn't help thinking—that one day you might have been mistress——"

"Of the windows? Then it's high time we turned our backs on them! That's just what I was thinking myself!"

CHAPTER XV.
THE INVISIBLE IDEAL.

On the flags of a London square, some days later, Ruth repeated the sigh that had succeeded on Gallow Hill, and once more Christina asked her what was the matter.

"I was thinking," said Ruth with a confidence born of the former occasion, "that one day all this, too, would have been more or less yours."

"All what, pray?"

"Every brick and slate that you can see! All this is part of the Dromard estate; they own every inch hereabouts."

Christina's next remark was a perfectly pleasant one in itself, only it referred to a totally different matter. And thus she treated poor Ruth. At other times she would herself rush into the subject without warning, and out of it the moment it wearied or annoyed her; to follow her closely in and out required a nimble tact indeed. Nor was it easy to know always the right thing to say, or at all delightful to feel that the right thing to-day might be the wrong thing to-morrow. But into this one subject Ruth was as ready to enter at a hint from Tiny as she was now contented to quit it at her caprice. The elder sister's patience and good temper were alike wonderful, but still more wonderful was her faith. Instinctively she felt that all was not over between Tiny and Lord Manister, and like many people who do not pretend to be clever, and are fond of saying so, she believed immensely in her instincts. It must not, however, be forgotten that her wishes for Tiny were the very best she could conceive; and it should be remembered that she had nobody but Tiny to watch over and care for, to think about and make plans for, during the long days when Erskine was in the City. This was the great excuse for Ruth, which never occurred to her husband, and was unknown even to herself. Christina was her baby, and a very troublesome, bad baby it was.

But what could you expect? The girl was sufficiently worried and unsettled; she was suffering from those upsetting fluctuations of mind which few of her kind entirely escape, but which are violent in characters that have grown with the emotional side to the sun and the intellectual side to the wall. In such a case the mind remains hard and green, while the emotions ripen earlier than need be; and the fault is the gardener's, and the gardener is the girl's mother. Now Mrs. Luttrell was a soulless but ladylike nonentity, with an eye naturally blind to the soul in her girls. All she herself had taught them was an unaffected manner and the necessity of becoming married. So Ruth had married both early and well by the favor of the gods, and Christina had restored the average by committing more follies of all sizes than would appear possible in the time. That in which Lord Manister was concerned had doubtless been the most important of the series, but its sting lay greatly in its notoriety. It had caused a light-hearted girl to see herself suddenly in the pupils of many eyes, and to recoil in shame from her own littleness. It had made her hate both herself and the owners of all those eyes, but men especially, of whom she had seen far too much in a short space of time. What she had done in England only heightened her poor opinion of herself now that it was done. She had seen her way to an incredibly sweet revenge, only to find it incredibly bitter. In striking hard she had hurt herself most, as Erskine had divined; instead of satisfying her naturally vindictive feeling toward Lord Manister that blow had killed it. Now she forgave him freely, but found it impossible to forgive herself; and so the generosity that was in a disordered heart asserted itself, because she had omitted to allow for it, not knowing it was there. Worse things asserted themselves too, such as the very solid attractions of the position which might have been hers; to these she could not help being fully alive, though this was one more reason why she hated herself. Her first judgment on herself, if a mere reaction at the beginning, became ratified and hardened as time went on. She became what she had never been before, even when notoriety had made her reckless—an introspective girl. And that made her twisty and queer and unaccountable; for, to be introspective with equanimity, you must have a bluff belief in yourself, which is not necessarily conceit, but Tiny was not blessed with it.

"She has lost her sense of fun—that's the worst part of the whole business!" exclaimed Erskine, one night when Christina had gone early to bed, as she always would now. "She has ceased to be amusing or easily amused. The empty town is boring her to the bone, and if I don't fix up our Lisbon trip we shall have her wanting to go back to Australia. However, I am bound to be in Lisbon by the end of next month, and I'm keener than ever on having you two with me. I know the ropes out there, and I could promise you both a good time—but that depends on Tiny. Let us hope the bay will blow the cobwebs out of her head; she wasn't made to be sentimental. I only wish I could get her to jeer at things as she used before we went to Essingham and while we were there!"

"Don't you think it's rather a good thing she has dropped that?" Ruth asked. "She had no respect for anything in those days."

"And her humor saved her! Pray what does she respect now?"

"Two or three people that I know of—my lord and master for one, and another person who is only a lord."

"Look here, Ruth, I don't believe it," cried Erskine, who by this time was pacing his study floor. "Why, she hasn't set eyes on him since the day she refused him—with variations."

"I know—but she's had time to reflect."

"Then I hope and pray she may never have the opportunity to recant!"

"Well, I won't deny that I hope differently," replied Ruth quietly; "but I've no reason to suppose there's any chance of it; and whatever happens, Erskine, you needn't be afraid of my—of my meddling any more."

"My dear girl, I know that," said he cordially enough; "but of course you tell her you're sorry for this, and you wish that. It's only natural that you should."

"Ah, I daren't say as much to her as you think," said Ruth, with a nod and a smile, for she was glad to know more than he did, here and there. "You needn't be afraid of me; I have little enough influence over her. She has only once opened her heart to me—once, and that's all."

Which was perfectly true, at the time.

But a few days later the restless girl was seized with a sudden desire to spend her money (which is really a good thing to do when you are troubled, if, like Christina, you have the money to spend), and as her most irregular desires were sure to be gratified by Ruth when they were not quite impossible, this whim was immediately indulged. It was rather late in the afternoon, but, on the other hand, the afternoon was extremely fine; and it was a Thursday, when men stay late in Lombard Street on account of next day's outward mails. Consequently there was no occasion for hurry; and so fascinated was Christina with the attractions and temptations of several well-known establishments, and last, as well as most of all, with those of the stores, that it was golden evening before they breathed again the comparatively fresh air of Victoria Street. It was like Christina to wish, at that hour, to walk home, and "through as many parks as possible"; it was even more like her to be extravagantly delighted with the first of these, and to insist on "shouting" Ruth a penny chair overlooking the ornamental water in St. James' Park.

Glad as she was to meet her sister's wishes, when she would only express them, which she was doing with inconvenient freedom this afternoon, Ruth did take exception to the penny chairs. Her feeling was that for the two of them to sit down solemnly on two of those chairs was not an entirely nice thing to do, and certainly not a thing that she would care to be seen doing. Knowing, however, that this would be no argument with Tiny, she merely said that it would make them too late in getting home; and that happened to be worse than none.

"Erskine said he wouldn't be home till eight o'clock; and he told us not to dress, as plain as he could speak," Tiny reminded her. "The other parks won't beat this; and you shall not be late, because I'll shout a hansom, too."

So Ruth made no more objections, though she felt a sufficient number; and they sat down with their eyes toward the pale traces of a gentle, undemonstrative September sunset, and were silent. Already the lamps were lighted in the Mall, where the trees were tanned and tattered by the change and fall of the leaf; at each end of the bridge, too, the lamps were lighted, and reflected below in palpitating pillars of fire; and every moment all the lights burnt brighter. Eastward a bluish haze mellowed trees and chimneys, making them seem more distant than they were; the noise of the traffic seemed more distant still, but it floated inward from the four corners, like the breaking of waves upon an islet; and here in the midst of it the stillness was strange, and certainly charming; only Tiny was immoderately charmed. She sat so long without speaking that Ruth leant back and watched her curiously. Her face was raised to the pale pink sky, with wide-opened eyes and tight-shut lips, as though the desires of her soul were written out in the tinted haze, as you may scratch with your finger in the bloom of a plum. She never spoke until the next quarter rang out from Westminster and was lingering in the quiet air, when she said, "Why have we never done this before, Ruth?"

"Well," answered Ruth, "I never did it myself before to-day; and I must own I think it's rather an odd thing to do."

"Ah, well, heaven may be odd—I hope it is!"

Ruth began to laugh. "My dear Tiny, you don't mean to say you call this heavenly?"

"It's near enough," said the young girl.

"But, my dear child, what stuff! The couples keep it sufficiently earthly, I should say—and the smell of bad tobacco, and that child's trumpet, and the midges and gnats—but principally 'Arry and 'Arriet."

"Now I just like to see them," said Christina, for once the serious person of the two, "they're so awfully happy."

"Awfully, indeed!" cried Ruth, with a superior little laugh. "Very vulgarly happy, I should say!" And Tiny did not immediately reply, but her eyes had fallen as far as the fretwork of the shabby foliage in the Mall, over which the sky still glowed; and when she spoke her words were the words of youthful speculation. She seemed, indeed, to be thinking aloud, and not at all sure of the sense of her thoughts.

"Very vulgarly happy!" she repeated, so long after the words had been spoken that it took Ruth some moments to recall them. "I am trying to decide whether there isn't something rather vulgar about all happiness of that kind—from the highest to the lowest. Forgive me, dear—I don't mean anything the least bit personal—I find I don't mean a word I've said! I wasn't thinking of the happiness itself so much, but of the desire for it. Oh, there must be something better for a girl to long for! There *is* something, if one only knew what it was; but nobody has ever shown me, for instance. Still there must be something between misery and marriage—something higher."

Her eyes had not fallen, but they shone with tears.

"I don't know anything higher than marrying the man you love," said Ruth honestly.

"Ah, if you love him! There is no need for *you* to know a higher happiness, even if one were possible in your case. But look at me!"

"You must marry, too," said Ruth with facility.

"As I probably shall; but to be happy, as you are happy, one ought to be fond of the person first, as you were; and—well, I don't think I have ever in my life felt as you felt."

"Stuff!" said Ruth, but with as much tenderness as the word would carry.

"I wish it were," returned Christina sadly; "it's the shameful truth. I have been going over things lately, and that's never a very cheerful employment in my case, but I think it has taught me my own heart this time. And I know now that I have never cared for anyone so much as for myself—much less for Lord Manister! If I had ever really cared for him I couldn't have treated him as I have done—no, not if he had behaved fifty times worse in the beginning. I was flattered by him, but I think I liked him, though I know I was dazzled by—the different things. I would have married him; I never loved him—nor any of the others!"

"Ah, well, Tiny, I am quite sure he loves you."

"Not very deeply, I hope; I can't altogether believe in him, and I don't much want to. It is bad enough to have one of them in deadly earnest," added Christina after a pause, but with a laugh.

"Is one of them—I mean another one?" asked Ruth, correcting herself quickly.

Tiny nodded. She would not say who it was. "I don't care for him either—not enough," she, however, vouchsafed.

"Then you don't think of marrying him, I hope?"

"No, not the man I mean"—she shook her head sadly at trees and sky—"I like him too much to marry him unless I loved him. Only if anyone else asked me—someone I didn't perhaps care a scrap for—I don't know what mightn't happen. I feel so reckless sometimes, and so sick of everything! This comes of having played at it so often that one is incapable of the real thing; more than all, it comes of growing up with no higher ideal than a happy marriage. And there must be something so much nobler—if one only knew what!"

Very wistfully her eyes wandered over the fading sky. The thin, floating clouds, fast disappearing in the darkness, were not less vague than her desires, and not more lofty. Her soul was tugging at a chain that had been too seldom taut.

"I know of nothing—unless you're a bluestocking," suggested poor Ruth, "or go in for Woman's Rights!"

Then the sights and sounds of the place came suddenly home to Christina, and her eyes fell. A child rattled by with an iron hoop. A pleasure boat, villainously rowed, passed with hoarse shouts through the pillar of fire below the bridge and left it writhing. Her eyes as she lowered them were greeted with the smarting smoke of a cigar, and her nostrils with the smell that priced it. The smoker took a neighboring chair, or rather two, for he was not without his companion.

Christina was the first to rise.

"I have been talking utter nonsense to you, Ruth," she whispered as they walked away; "but it was kind of you to let me go on and on. One has sometimes to say a lot more than one means to get out a little that one does mean; you must try to separate the little from the lot. I've been talking on tiptoe—it was good of you not to push me over!"

They crossed the bridge, throbbing beneath the tread of many feet; in the Mall, under the half-clothed trees, they hailed a hansom, and Ruth greeted her reflection in the side mirror with a sigh of relief.

"We should never have done this if we hadn't been Australians," she remarked, as though exceedingly ashamed of what they had done, as indeed she was.

"Then that's one more good reason for thanking Heaven we *are* Australians!" answered Tiny, with some of her old spirit. "You may think differently, Ruth, but for my part that's the one point on which I have still some lingering shreds of pride."

And that was how Tiny Luttrell opened her heart a second time to Ruth, her sister, who was of less comfort to her even than before, because now her open heart was also the cradle of a waking soul. More things than one need name, for they must be obvious, had of late worked together toward this awakening, until now the soul tossed and struggled within a frivolous heart, and its cries were imperious, though ever inarticulate. To Ruth they were but faint echoes of the unintelligible; scarce hearing, she was contented not to try to understand. When Tiny said she had been "talking on tiptoe," to Ruth's mind that merely expressed a queer mood queerly. She did not see how accurately it figured the young soul straining upward; indeed the accuracy was unconscious, and Christina herself did not see this.

Queer as it may have been, her mood had made for nobility, and was, therefore, memorable among the follies and worse of which, unhappily, she was still in the thick. It passed from her not to return, yet to lodge, perhaps, where all that is good in our lives and hearts must surely gather and remain until the spirit itself goes to complete and to inhabit a new temple, and we stand built afresh in the better image of God.

CHAPTER XVI.
FOREIGN SOIL.

There is in Cintra a good specimen of the purely Portuguese hotel, which is worth a trial if you can speak the language of the country and eat its meats; if you want to feel as much abroad as you are, this is the spot to promote that sensation. The whole concern is engagingly indigenous. They will give you a dinner of which every course (there must be nearly twenty) has the twofold charm of novelty and mystery combined; and you shall dine in a room where it is safe, if unsportsmanlike, to criticise aloud your fellow-diners, when their ways are most notably not your ways. Then, after dinner, you may make music in a pleasant drawing room or saunter in the quaint garden behind the hotel; only remember that the garden has a view which is necessarily lost at night.

The view is good, and it improves as the day wears on by reason of the beetling crag that stands between Cintra and the morning sun. So close is this crag to the town, and so sheer, that at dawn it looms the highest mountain on earth; but with the afternoon sunlight streaming on its face you see it for what it is, and there is much in the sight to satisfy the eye. Halfway up the vast wall is forested with fir trees picked out with bright villas and streaked with the white lines of ascending roads. The upper portion is of granite, rugged and bare and iron gray. The topmost angle is surmounted by square towers and battlements that seem a part of the peak, as indeed they are, since the Moors who made them hewed the stones from the spot; and the serrated crest notches the sky like a crown on a hoary head. Finer effects may recur very readily to the traveled eye, but to one too used to flat regions this is fine enough: thus Tiny Luttrell was in love with Cintra from the moment when she and Ruth and Erskine first set foot in the garden of the Portuguese hotel, and let their eyes climb up the sunlit face of the rock.

They were a merrier party now than when leaving Plymouth. They had left fog and damp behind them (it was near the end of October), and steamed back to summer in a couple of days; and that alone was inspiriting. Then they had already stayed a day or two in Lisbon, where Erskine had spent as many years when Ruth was an infant at the other end of the world, so that he was naturally a good guide. There, too, Ruth and Tiny made some friends, being charmingly treated by people with whom they were unable to converse, while Erskine attended to the business matter which had brought him over. The girls were not sorry to hear that this matter was hanging fire, as such matters have a way of doing in Lisbon, for they were enjoying themselves thoroughly. Ruth felt prouder than ever of her big husband when she saw him among his Portuguese friends, and she thought him very clever to speak their language so fluently. As for Tiny, she seemed herself again; she was willing to be amused, and luckily there was much to amuse her. Much, on the other hand, she could seriously admire, and her high opinion of Portugal was itself amusing after the fault she had found with another country; she even made comparisons between the two, which gave considerable pleasure when translated by Erskine. Cintra pleased her most, however. She delighted in the hotel, where there were no English tongues but their own; she even pretended to enjoy the dinner. So Erskine felt proud of his choice of quarters; only he missed his English paper, and had to go to the English hotel and purchase unnecessary refreshment on the chance of a glimpse of one. Your man-Briton abroad is miserable without that. It is a male weakness entirely. Holland took with him on that pilgrimage no sympathy from the ladies, who only derided him when he came back confessing that he had thrown his money away, as some other fellow was staying at the English inn and reading the paper in his room.

"But I'm very sorry there's another Englishman in the place," announced Christina; "though I suppose one ought to be thankful he didn't choose our hotel. It is something like being abroad, staying here; one more Englishman would have spoilt the fun."

"When you see the steeds I've ordered for the morning," said Erskine, with a laugh, "you'll feel more abroad than ever."

And they did, indeed, when the morning came; for their steeds were three small asses in charge of a dark-eyed child who was whacking them for his amusement while he smoked a cigarette. A small but picturesque crowd had collected in the street to see the start, and were greatly entertained by the spectacle of the Senhor Inglez (a giant among them) astride a donkey little taller than a big dog. Interest was also shown in the camera legs, which Erskine carried like a lance in rest, while the camera itself was nursed by Christina, who had spoilt a power of plates in Lisbon without becoming discouraged. The small boy threw away his cigarette, and having asked Erskine for another, which was sternly denied him, smote each donkey in turn and set the cavalcade in motion.

They passed the palace in the little market place, and were unable to admire it; they passed the loathly prison, which is the worst feature of Cintra, and were duly abused by the prisoners at the barred windows; they were glad to reach the outskirts of the town, and to begin their ascent of the rock up which their eyes had already climbed. They were to devote the day to the ruined Moorish fort they had seen against the sky, and to the Palace of Pena, which stands on a peak hidden from the town; and Erskine, who was confident that they were all going to enjoy themselves very particularly, declared that the day was only worthy of the cause. There was not a cloud in the sky, and the weather was just warm enough for the work in hand. As the donkeys wended their way up the steep roads, Mr. Holland was advised to get off and carry his carrier; but he knew the Cintra donkey of old, and sat ignobly still. He also knew the Cintra donkey boy, and aired his Portuguese upon the attendant imp, who passed on the way, and greeted with jeers, a professional friend waiting with only one donkey in front of a pretty house overlooking the road.

"Ah," said Erskine, "that's the English hotel; and no doubt that moke is for the opposition Senhor Inglez—whose name is Jackson."

"Then pray let us push on," cried Christina anxiously. "Do you suppose he is coming our way, Erskine?"

"Most probably, to begin with; but he may turn off for Monserrat or the cork convent."

"Let us hope so. If he should pass us, Erskine, just talk Portuguese to us as loud as ever you can!"

"Far better to hurry up and not be overtaken," added Ruth, who was thinking of her appearance, with which she was far from satisfied.

Accordingly the imp (with whose good looks Christina had already expressed herself as enamored) was employed for some moments at his favorite occupation. But for the pursuing Englishman, however, Tiny, instead of leading the way upward, would have dismounted more than once to set up her camera; for low parapets were continually on their left, high walls on their right; and wherever there was a gap in the fir trees growing below the parapets, a fresh view was presented of the town below. First it was a bird's-eye view of the palace, seen to better advantage through the trees of the Rua de Duque Saldanha than before, from the street; then a fair impression of the town as a whole, with its gay gardens and cheap looking stuccoed houses; and then successive editions of Cintra, each one smaller than the last, and each with a wider tract of undulating brown land beyond, and a broader band of ocean at the horizon. Then they plunged into mountain gorges; there were no more distant views, but mighty walls on either side, and reddening foliage interlacing overhead, as though woven upon the strip of pure blue sky. And the atmosphere was clear as distilled water in a crystal vessel; but in the shade the air had a sweet keenness, an inspiriting pungency, under whose influence the enthusiast of the party grew inevitably eloquent in the praises of Portugal.

"I can't tell you how I like it!" she said to Erskine, with a color on her cheeks and a light in her eyes which alone seemed worth the voyage. "I call it a real good country, which has never had justice done to it. If I could write I would boom it. Of course I haven't seen Italy or Switzerland, nor yet France, but I have seen England. If I were condemned to live in Europe at all, I'd rather live at this end of it than at yours, Erskine. Look at the climate—it's as good as our Australian climate, and very like it—and this is all but November. You have no such air in England, even in summer, but when you think of what we left behind us the other day, it's ditch water unto wine compared with this. Ah, what a day it is, and what a place, and how fresh and queer and un-English the whole thing is!"

"I am perhaps spoiling it for you," suggested Erskine apologetically, "by being not un-English myself?"

"No, Erskine, it's only me you're spoiling," returned the girl unexpectedly, and with a grateful smile for Ruth as well. "But I don't know another Briton—home or colonial—who wouldn't rather spoil the day and the place for me."

"That's a pity, because I happen to smell the blood of an Englishman at this moment—at least I hear his donkey."

They stopped to listen, and following hoofs were plainly audible.

"Then he hasn't turned off for the other places!" exclaimed Ruth, smoothing her skirt.

Erskine shrugged his shoulders like a native of the country. "No, he is evidently bound for our port; and as the chances are that he is under sixteen stone, he's sure to overtake us. It is I that am keeping you all back."

"We won't look round," exclaimed Tiny decisively; "and you shall shout at us in Portuguese as he comes up, and we'll say 'Sim, Senhor!'"

So they kept their eyes most rigorously in front of them; and such was the authority of Tiny that Erskine was in the midst of an absurd speech in Portuguese when they were overtaken. That harangue was interrupted by the voice of the interloping Englishman; and was never resumed, as the voice was Lord Manister's.

The meeting was plainly an embarrassing one for all concerned, but it had at least the appearance of a very singular coincidence; and nothing will go further in conversation than the slightest or most commonplace coincidence. You must be very nervous indeed if you are incapable of expressing your surprise, of which much may be made, while the little bit of personal history to follow need not entail a severe intellectual effort. Lord Manister accounted very simply, if a little eagerly, for his presence in Portugal; he went on to explain that he had heard much of Cintra, but not, as he was glad to find, one word too much. Personally, he was delighted and charmed. Was not Mrs. Holland charmed and delighted? It was at Ruth's side that Lord Manister rode forward, falling into the position very naturally indeed.

Quite as naturally the other two dropped behind. "So now I suppose your day will be spoilt, Tiny," murmured Erskine, with a wry smile.

"The day is doomed—unless he has the good taste to see he isn't wanted."

"Well, I wouldn't let him see that, even if he does bore you," said Erskine, who had his doubts on this point. "I don't think he's looking very well," he added meditatively.

As for Christina, she was staring fixedly at Lord Manister's back; for once, however, his excellent attire earned no gibe from her; and while she was still seeking for some more convincing mode of parading her immutable indifference toward that young man, a turn in the road brought them suddenly before the gates of Pena. The four closed up and rode through the gates abreast; and, presently dismounting, they left their small steeds to the sticks of the Cintra donkey boys, and walked together up the broad, sloping path.

"By the way," remarked Holland, "I was told there was only one other Englishman in Cintra at the moment—a man of the name of Jackson; have you arrived this morning?"

"I am afraid—I'm Jackson!" confessed Manister, with a blush and a noisy laugh.

"Oh, I see," said Mr. Holland, laughing also; and he saw a good deal.

"Of course you have to do that sometimes; I can quite understand it," Ruth said in a sympathetic voice. "Still I think we must call you Mr. Jackson!" she added slyly.

Christina said nothing at all. Her extreme silence and self-possession hardly tended to promote the common comfort; her only comment on Lord Manister's alias was a somewhat scornful smile. As they all pressed upward by well-kept paths, in the shadow of tall fir trees, she kept assiduously by Erskine's side. The ascent, however, was steep enough to touch the breath, and conversation was for some minutes neither a pleasure nor a necessity. Then, above the firs, the palace of Pena reared hoary head and granite shoulders; for, like the ruined fort visible from the town below, the palace is built upon the summit of a rock. Still a steeper climb, and the party stood looking down upon the fir trees which had just shadowed them, with their backs to the palace walls, that seem, and often are, a part of the rugged peak itself. For this is a palace not only founded on a rock, and on the rock's topmost crag, but the foundation has itself supplied so many features ready-made that nature and the Moors may be said to have collaborated in its making. Three of the party, having taken breath, played catch with this idea; but Christina barely listened. Her attitude was regrettable, but not unnatural.

In the last place on earth where she would have expected to meet anyone she knew, she had met the last person whom she expected to meet anywhere. She remembered telling him of her mooted trip to Portugal with the Hollands, she remembered also his telling her to be sure to go to Cintra; her recollection of the conversation in question, and of Lady Almeric's conservatory, where it had taken place, was sufficiently clear, now that she thought of it; but certainly she had never thought of it since. Had he? She might have mentioned the time when the trip was likely to take place; she was not so sure of this, but it seemed likely; and in that case, was a certain explanation of his sojourn in Portugal, other than the explanation he had been so careful to give, either preposterous in itself or the mere suggestion of her own vanity?

These questions were now worrying Christina as she had seldom been worried before, even about Lord Manister, who had been much in her thoughts for many weeks past. Yet Manister was not the only person on her mind at the moment. Just before leaving London she had experienced the fulfillment of a prophecy, by receiving from Countess Dromard a stare as stony as the pavement they met on, which was near enough to Piccadilly to inspire a superstitious respect for sibylline Mrs. Willoughby. In the disagreeable moment following Tiny's thoughts had flown straight to that lady—indeed her only remark at the time had been "Good old Mrs. Willoughby!" to which Ruth (who suffered at Tiny's side, and for her part turned positively faint with mortification) had been in no condition to reply. Little as she showed it, however, Christina had felt the affront far more keenly than Ruth—chiefly because she took it all to herself, and was unable to think it utterly undeserved. In any event she felt it now. It was but the other day that the countess had cut her. The wound was still tender; the sight of Lord Manister scrubbed it cruelly. And long afterward the scar had its own little place among the forces driving Christina in a certain direction, whether she went on feeling it or not.

Hardly less preoccupied than herself was the man whose side Christina would not leave. Wherefore, though the place was old ground to him, as a guide he was instructive rather than amusing. He spoke the requisite Portuguese to the janitors, whose stock facts he also translated into intelligible English; he led the way up the winding staircase of the round tower, and from the giddy gallery at the top he did not omit to point out Torres Vedras and such like landmarks; descending, he had stock facts of his own connected with chapel and sacristy, but he failed to make them interesting. A paid guide could not have been more perfunctory in method, though it is certain that the most entertaining showmanship would have failed to entertain Erskine's hearers, each one of whom was more or less nervous and ill at ease. He himself was thinking only of Christina, who would not leave his side. He saw her watching Lord Manister; though she would hardly speak to him, he saw pity in her glance. He heard Lord Manister talking volubly to Ruth; he did not know about what, and he wondered if Manister knew, himself. Erskine did not understand. The girl seemed to care, and if she did—if this thing was to be—he would never say another word against it. If she cared there would not be another word to say, save in joyous and loving congratulation. That was the whole question: whether she cared. For the first time Erskine was not sure; it was a toss-up in his mind whether Tiny was sure herself. Certainly there seemed to be hope for the man who was being watched yet avoided; however, Erskine was resolved to give him the very first opportunity of learning his fate.

Accordingly he reminded Tiny that he had been carrying the camera ever since they had dismounted: and was his arm to ache for nothing? The suggestion of the square tower, with the steps below, as an admirable target, also came from Erskine. Lord Manister helped to take the photograph. That, again, was Erskine's doing; and he even did more. When they all turned their backs on Pena, and their faces to the ruin on the opposite peak, it was her husband who rode ahead with Ruth. His reward was the smile of an angel over a lost soul saved. He returned the smile cynically. But round the first corner he belabored his ass with the camera legs, and shot ahead, Ruth gladly following.

In the hollow between the peaks the bridle path passes an ancient and picturesque mosque, with a lime tree growing in the center; from this the ruin derives a roof in summer, a carpet in winter, and had now a little of each.

"What a romantic place!" said Ruth, peeping in. Her husband had waited for her to do so.

"Then let us leave it to more romantic people," he answered, dropping the tripod in the doorway. "They may like to have a photograph of it—for every reason! You and I had better climb up to the fort and chuck stones into Cintra till they come."

This looked quite possible when at last they sat perched upon the antique battlements; they seemed so to overhang the little town. Erskine lit a Portuguese cigarette, which the wind finished for him in a minute. Ruth kept a hand upon her hat. Then she spoke out, with the wind whistling between their faces.

"Erskine, I know what you think—that this isn't an accident!"

"Of course it isn't."

"And I dare say you think *I* have had something to do with it?"

"Have you, I wonder? You may easily have said that we thought of coming here—quite innocently, you know."

"Then I never said so at all. I thought—you know what I thought would have happened last August. Erskine, I have had absolutely nothing to do with it this time!"

"My dear, you needn't say that. I know neither you nor Tiny have had anything to do with it—so far as you are aware; but Tiny must have told him we were coming here, and this is his roundabout dodge of seeing her again. Certainly that looks as if he were in earnest."

"I always said he was."

"And as for Tiny, I don't pretend to make her out. You see, they do not come. I shouldn't be surprised at anything."

"No more should I; but I should be thankful. Even when I hid things from you, Erskine, I never pretended I shouldn't be thankful if this happened, did I? Oh, and you'll be thankful, too, when you see them happy—as we are happy!"

Holland sat for some minutes with bent head, picking lichen from granite.

"My dear girl," he said at length, and tenderly, "don't let us talk any more about it. I dare say I have taken a rotten view of it all along. I only thought—that he didn't deserve her, and that neither of them could care enough. It seems I was more or less wrong; but there is nothing further to be said until we know."

He leant over the battlements, gazing down into the toy town below. Ruth brooked his silence for a time. Then he heard her saying:

"They are a very long while. He's certainly helping her to take a photograph."

"I hope he'll get a negative," said Erskine, with a laugh.

They came at last.

"How long have you been there, Erskine?" shouted Tiny from below. She held one end of the tripod, by which Manister was tugging her uphill.

"About ten minutes."

"Not as much, Erskine," said Ruth.

"We have been photographing that charming mosque," Manister said, as he set down the camera and wiped his forehead; "you meant us to, didn't you, Holland?"

"Of course I did."

"And have you got a negative?" asked poor Ruth.

"A month to make up her mind!" cried Erskine Holland, on hearing at second hand what had actually happened in the mosque. "No wonder he wouldn't stay and dine, and no wonder he is going back to Lisbon to-morrow. By Jove! he *must* be fond of her to stand it at all. To go and wait a month!"

"He offered to wait six," said Ruth.

"Then he's a fool," said Erskine quietly. "Tell me, Ruth, is it a thing one may speak about? One would like, of course, to say something pleasant. After all, it's very like an engagement, and I could at least tell her that I like him. I did like him to-day. Under the circumstances he behaved capitally; only I do think him a fool not to have insisted on her deciding one way or the other."

"I don't think I'd mention the matter unless she does," Ruth said doubtfully. "She told me to tell you she would rather not speak of it at present. You see she has thought of you already! She says you will find her the same as ever if only you will try to look as though you didn't know anything about it. She declares that she means to make the most of her time for the next month wherever she may be, and she hopes you have ordered the donkeys for to-morrow. Still she is troubled, and if she thought you didn't disapprove—if she thought you approved—I can see that it would make a difference to her. She thinks so much of your opinion—only she doesn't want to speak to you herself about this until it is a settled thing. But if you would send her your blessing, dear, I know she would appreciate that."

"Then take it to her by all means," said Erskine, heartily enough. "Tell her I think she is very wise to have left it open—you needn't say what I think of Manister for letting her do so. But you may say, if she likes to hear it, that I think him a jolly good fellow, who will make her very happy if she can really feel she cares for him. Tell her it all hangs on that. That's what we have to impress upon her, and you're the proper person to do so. I only felt one ought to say something pleasant. Wait a moment—tell her I'll do my best to give her a good time until December if none of us are ever to have one again!"

Tiny was sitting at the dressing table in her room, slowly and deliberately burning a photograph in the flame of a candle. The photograph was on a yellow mount which Ruth remembered, and as she drew near Tiny turned it face downward to the flame, which smacked still more of a former occasion.

"Tiny!" cried Ruth in alarm, laying her hand on the young girl's shoulder. "What on earth are you burning, dear?"

"My boats," replied Christina grimly; and turning the photograph over, the face of Jack Swift was still uncharred.

"So you've carried *his* photograph with you all this time?"

"He is as good a friend as I shall ever have."

"Then why burn him if he is only a friend?"

"Perhaps he would like to be more; and perhaps there was once a moment when he might have been. But now I shall duly marry Lord Manister—if he has patience."

"Then why keep poor Lord Manister in suspense, Tiny, dearest?"

"Because I'm not in love with him; and I question whether he's as much in love with me as he imagines—I told him so."

"As it is, you may find it difficult to draw back."

"Exactly; so I am burning my boats. Jack, my dear, that's the last of you!"

Her voice satisfied Ruth, who, however, could see no more of her face than the curve of her cheek, and beyond it the blackened film curling from the burning cardboard.

CHAPTER XVII.
THE HIGH SEAS.

"He's done it at last!"

Erskine brandished a letter as he spoke, and then leant back in his chair with a guffaw that alarmed the Portuguese waiters. The letter was from Herbert Luttrell, a Cambridge man of one month's standing, of whose academic outset too little had been heard. His sisters were anxious to know what it was that he had done at last; they put this question in the same breath.

"Oh, it might be worse," said Erskine cheerfully. "He has stopped short of murder!"

"We should like to know how far he got," Tiny said, while Ruth held out an eager hand for the letter.

"I don't think you must read it, my dear; but the fact is he has at last filled up somebody's eye!"

Tiny breathed a sigh of relief.

"Is he in prison?" asked Ruth.

"No, not yet; but I am afraid he must be in bad odor, though perhaps not with everybody."

"Whose was the eye?" Christina wanted to know.

"The proctor's!" suggested Ruth.

"Not yet, again—you must give the poor boy time, my dear. It may be the proctor's turn next, but at present your little brother has contented himself with filling the eye of the man who was coaching his college trials. It's a time-honored privilege of the coach to use free language to his crew, and it doesn't give offense as a rule; but it seems to have offended Herbert. Young Australia don't like being sworn at, and Herbert admits that he swore back from his thwart, and said that he fancied he was as good a man as the coach, but he hoped to find out when they got to the boathouse. They did find out; and Herbert has at last filled up an old country eye; and for my part I don't think the less of him for doing so."

"The less!" cried Tiny, whose blue eyes were alight. "*I* think all the more of him. I'm proud of Herbs! You have too many of those savage old customs, Erskine; you need Young Australia to come and knock them on the head!"

"Well, as long as he doesn't knock a proctor on the head, as Ruth seems to fear! If he does that there's an end of him, so far as Cambridge is concerned. He tells me the eye was unpopular, otherwise I'm afraid he would have had a warm time of it; though a quick fist and an arm that's stronger than it looks are wonderful things for winning the respect of men, even in these days."

"And mayn't we really see the letter?" Tiny said wistfully.

Erskine shook his head.

"I am very sorry, but I'm afraid I must treat it as private. It's a verbatim report. I can only tell you that Herbert seems to have been justified, more or less, though he is perhaps too modest to report himself as fully as he reports the eye. He says nothing else of any consequence. He doesn't mention work of any kind; but he's not there only, or even primarily, to pass exams. On the whole, we mustn't fret about the eye, so long as the dear boy keeps his hands off the authorities."

Their hotel was no longer at Cintra, but in Lisbon, where Mr. Holland was being sadly delayed by the business men of the most unbusinesslike capital in Europe. Already it was the middle of November. They had left Cintra as long ago as the 5th of the month, expecting to sail from Lisbon on the 7th; but out of his experience Erskine ought to have known better. It is true that on landing in the country he had attended first to business. The business was connected with the forming of a company for certain operations on Portuguese territory in the East, the capital coming from London; a board was necessary in both cities, and very necessary indeed were certain negotiations between the London directors, as represented by Erskine Holland, and their colleagues in Lisbon. The latter had promised to do much while Erskine was at Cintra, and duly did nothing until he returned; knowing their kind of old, he ought never to have gone. He quite deserved to have to wait and worry and smoke more Portuguese cigarettes than were either agreeable or good, with the women on his hands; with all his knowledge of the country and the people he might have known very well how it would be—as indeed Erskine was told in a letter from Lombard Street, where an amusing dispatch of his from Cintra had rather irritated the senior partners.

Thus Mr. Holland had his own worries throughout this trip, but it is a pleasure to affirm that his sister-in-law did not add to them after that first day at Cintra. Thenceforward she had behaved herself as a perfectly rational and even a contented being. She had appreciated the other sights of Cintra even more than Pena (which had hardly been given a fair chance), and most of all that gorgeous garden of Monserrat, where the trees of the world are grouped together, and among them the gum trees which were so dear to Christina. She had even been overcome by a bloodthirsty desire to witness the bullfight on the Sunday; and Erskine had taken her, because her present frame was not one to discourage; but it must be confessed that Tiny was disappointed by the tameness of this sport rather than revolted by its cruelty. Negatively, she had been behaving better still; the Cintra donkey, the locality of the English hotel, and other associations of the first day never once perceptibly affected either her spirits or her temper. She had shown, indeed, so dead a level of cheerfulness and good sense as to seem almost uninteresting after the accustomed undulations; but in point of fact she had never been more interesting to those in her secret. She had promised to give Lord Manister his answer in a month, and meanwhile she was displaying all the even temper and equable spirits of settled happiness. She ate healthily, she declared that she slept well, and otherwise she was amazingly and consistently serene. That was her perversity, once more, but on this occasion her perversity admitted of an obvious explanation. The explanation was that she had never been in doubt about her decision, that in her heart she was more than satisfied, and that she had asked for a month's respite chiefly for freedom's sake. The matter was discussed no more between the sisters, because Tiny refused to discuss it, declaring that she had dismissed it from her mind till December. And to Erskine she never once mentioned it while they were in Portugal, nor had she the least intention of doing so on the homeward voyage, which they were able ultimately to make within a week of the arrival of Herbert's letter.

But the voyage was rough, and Tiny happened to be a remarkably good sailor, which made her very tiresome once more. Holland had his hands full in attending to his wife in the cabin, while keeping an eye on her sister, who would remain on deck. Through the worst of the weather the unreasonable girl clung like a limpet to the rail, staring seaward at the misty horizon, or downward at the milky wake, until her pale face was red and rough and sparkling with dried spray.

"I do wish you would come below," Erskine said to her, in a tone of entreaty, toward dusk on the second day, but by no means for the first time. "There's not another woman on deck; and you've chosen the one spot of the whole vessel where there's most motion."

Until he joined her Tiny had indeed been the only soul on the hurricane deck, where she stood, leaning on the after-rail, with eyes for nothing but the steamer's track. They were on the hem of the bay and the wind was ahead, so the boat was pitching; and you must be a good sailor to enjoy leaning over the after-rail with this motion—but that is what Christina was. The wind welded her garments to the wire network underneath, and loosened her hair, and lit lamps in her ears; but it seemed that she liked it, and that the long, frothy trail had a strong fascination for her; for when she answered, it was without lifting her eyes from the sea.

"You see, I like being different from other people; that's what I go in for! Honestly, though, I love being up here, and I think you might let me stay.

However, that's no reason why you should stay too—if it makes you feel uncomfortable."

"Thanks, I think I am proof," returned Erskine rather brusquely, for this is a point on which most men are either vain or sensitive; "but of course I'll leave you, if you prefer it."

"On the contrary, I should like you to stay," Christina murmured—in such a lonely little voice that Erskine stayed.

It was difficult to believe in this young lady's sincerity, however. She not only made no further remark herself, but refused to acknowledge one of Erskine's. Men do not like that, either. Tiny's eyes had never been lifted from the endless race of white water, now rising as though to their feet, now sinking from under them as the steamer labored end on to the wind. Apparently she had forgotten that Erskine was there, as also that she had asked him to remain. He was on the point of leaving her to her reverie when she swung round suddenly, with only one elbow on the rail, and looked up at him with a pout that turned slowly to a smile.

"Erskine, you've come and spoilt everything!"

"My dear child, I told you I would go if you liked, you know."

"Ah, that was too late; you'd spoilt it then. It won't come back."

"Do you mean that I have broken some spell? If that's the case I am very sorry."

"That won't mend it—you can't mend spells," said Tiny, laughing ruefully. "Perhaps it's as well you can't; and perhaps it's a good thing you came," she added more briskly. "I had humbugged myself into thinking I was on my way back to Australia. That was all."

"But if I were to go mightn't you humbug yourself again?"

"I don't think I want to," the girl answered thoughtfully; "at any rate I don't want you to go. Don't you think it's jolly up here? To me it's as good as a gallop up the bush—and I think we're taking our fences splendidly! But it was jollier still thinking that England was over there," nodding her head at the wake, "and that every five minutes or so it was a mile further away—instead of the other thing."

"Poor old England!"

"No, Erskine, I meant a mile nearer Australia—that was the jolly feeling," Tiny made haste to explain. "You know I didn't mean anything else—you know how I have enjoyed being with you and Ruth. Only I can't help wishing

I was on my way back to Melbourne instead of to Plymouth. I'd give so much to see Australia again."

"Well, so you will see it again."

Her eyes sped seaward as she shook her head.

"Why on earth shouldn't you?" said Erskine, laughing.

"You know why."

Now he saw her meaning, and held his tongue. This was the subject on which he understood it to be her desire that they should not speak. To himself, moreover, it was a highly unattractive topic, and he was thoroughly glad to have it ignored as it had been; but if she alluded to the matter herself that was another thing, and he must say something. So he said:

"Is it really so certain, Tiny?"

"On my part absolutely. I'm only climbing down!"

Erskine was reminded of the pleasant things he had thought of saying to her at Cintra; they had been by him so long that he found himself saying them now as though he meant every word.

"My congratulations must keep till the proper time; but when that comes they may surprise you. My dear girl, I should like you to understand that you're not the only person whose opinion has changed since we were at Essingham. If I may say so at this stage of the proceedings, and if it is any satisfaction to you to hear it, I for one am going to be very glad about this thing, I think him such a first-rate fellow, Tiny!"

For a moment Christina gazed acutely at her brother-in-law. "I wonder if that's sincere?" she said reflectively. Then her eyes hurried back to the sea.

"I think he's a very good fellow indeed," said Erskine with emphasis.

The girl gave a little laugh. "Oh, he's all that; the question is whether that's enough."

"It is, if he really loves you—as I think he must."

"Oh, if it's enough for him to be in love!"

There followed a great pause, during which the thought of pleasant things to say was thrown overboard and left far astern.

"I only hope," Erskine said at last, with an earnest ring in his voice which was new to Christina, "that you are not going to make the greatest mistake of your life!"

"I hope not also."

"Ah, don't make light of it!" he cried impetuously. "If you marry without love you'll ruin your life, I don't care who it is you marry! To marry for affection, or for esteem, or for money—they're all equally bad; there is no distinction. Take affection—for a time you might be as happy as if it were something more; but remember that any day you might see somebody that you could really love. Then you would know the difference, and it would embitter your whole existence with a quiet, private, unsuspected bitterness, of which you can have no conception. And so much the worse if you have married somebody who is honestly and sufficiently fond of you. His love would cut you to the heart—because you could only pretend to return it—because your whole existence would be a living lie!"

He was extremely unlike himself. His voice trembled, and in the dying light his face was gray. These things made his words impressive, but the girl did not seem particularly impressed. Had she remembered the one previous occasion when a similar conversation had taken place between them, the strangeness of his manner must have been driven home to her by contrast; but the contrast was a double one, and her own share in it kept her from thinking of the time when she had been serious and he had not, and now, when he was more serious than she had ever known him, she met him with a frivolous laugh.

"Well, really, Erskine, I've never heard you so terribly in earnest before! I think I had better not tell Ruth what you have said; my dear man, you speak as though you'd been there!"

It was some time before he laughed.

"If only you yourself would be more in earnest, Tiny! You may say this comes badly from me. I know there has been more jest than earnest between me and you. But if I was never serious in my life before I am now, and I want you, too, to take yourself seriously for once. You see, Tiny, I am not only an old married man by this time, but I am your European parent as well. I am entitled to play the heavy father, and to give you a lecture when I think you need one. My dear child, I have been in the world about twice as long as you have, and I know men and have heard of women who have poisoned their whole lives by marrying with love on the other side only; and the greater their worldly goods, the greater has been their misery! And rather than see you do as they have done——" The sentence snapped. "You shan't do it!" he exclaimed sharply. "You're far too good to spoil yourself as others have done and are doing every day."

"Who told you I was good?" inquired Christina, with a touch of the coquetry which even with him she could not entirely repress. "You never had it from me, most certainly. Let me tell you, Erskine, that I'm bad—bad—bad! And if I haven't shocked you sufficiently already it is evidently time that I did; so you'll please to understand that if I marry Lord Manister it is partly because I think I owe it to him; otherwise it's for the main chance purely. And I think it's very unkind of you to make me confess all this," she added fretfully. "I never meant to speak to you about it at all. Only I can't bear you to think me better than I am."

Erskine shook his head sadly.

"At least you have a better side than this, Tiny—this is not you at all! You love and admire all that is honest and noble, and fresh and free; you should give that love and admiration a chance. But I'm not going to say any more to worry you. If you really, with your eyes open, are going to marry a man whom you do not love, I can only tell you that you will be doing at best a very cynical thing. And yet—I can understand it." This he added more to himself than to the girl.

He was turning away, but she laid a restraining hand upon his arm.

"Don't go," she exclaimed impulsively. "I can't let you go when—when you understand me better than anyone else ever did—and when I am never, never going to speak to you like this again."

"If only I could help you!"

"You cannot!" Tiny cried out. "I'm too far gone to be helped. I feel hopelessly bad and hard, and nobody can mend that. But if there's one grain of goodness in my composition that wasn't there when I came over to England, you may know, Erskine, if you care to know it, that it's you, and you alone, who have put it there!"

"Nonsense," he said; "what good have I done you?"

"You have talked sense to me, as only one other man ever did—and he wasn't as clever as you are. You've given me books to read, and they're the first good books I ever read in my life; you have dug a sort of oyster knife into my miserable ignorance! You have been a real good pal to me, Erskine, and you must never turn your back on me, whatever I do. I know you never will. I believe in you as I believe in very few people on this footstool; but there's one thing you can do for me now that will be even kinder than anything that you have ever done yet."

"There's nothing that I wouldn't do for you, Tiny," said Erskine tenderly. "What is it?"

The corners of her mouth twitched—her eyes twinkled.

"It's not to say another serious word to me this month! I know I began it this time; I won't do so again. I'm trying to be happy in my own way, if you'll only let me. I'm trying to make the most of my time. When I'm really engaged I shall need all the help and advice you can give me; for I mean to be very good to him, Erskine; I do indeed! Then of course I shall need to cultivate the finest manners; but until it actually comes off I'm trying to forget about it—don't you see? I'm doing my level best to forget!"

What Erskine saw was the tears in her eyes, but he saw them only for an instant; instead of his leaving Christina on the deck it was she who left him; and there he stood, between the high seas and the gathering shades of night, until both were black.

It was their last conversation of the kind.

One more night was spent at sea; the next they were all back in Kensington. Here they were greeted with a pleasant surprise: Herbert was in the house to meet them. Cambridge seemed already to have done him good; he was singularly polite and subdued, though a little uncommunicative. They, however, had much to tell him, so this was not noticed immediately. His sisters supposed that he was in London for the night only, as he said he had come down from Cambridge that day. It was not until later that they knew that he had been sent down. Erskine broke the news to them.

"I'm afraid," he added, "that they've sent him down for good and all. The fact is, Ruth, your fears have been realized. He has done his best to fill another eye; and this time the proctor's! He says he shall go back to Melbourne immediately."

"Never!" cried Ruth; and she went straight to her brother, who was smoking viciously in another room.

"Yes, by ghost!" drawled Herbert through his hooked nose. "I'm going to clear out. I'm full up of England, Ruth, and I guess England's full up of me. The best thing I can do is to go back, and turn boundary rider or whim driver. That's about all I'm fit for, and it's what I'm going to do. The *Ballaarat* sails on the 2d—I've been to the office and taken my berth already. My oath, I drove there straight from Liverpool Street this afternoon!"

Nor was there any moving him from his purpose, though Ruth tried for half an hour there and then. Twice that time Herbert spent afterward in Tiny's room; but it was not known whether Tiny also had attempted to dissuade him. When he left her the girl stood for five minutes with a foot on the fender and an elbow on the mantelpiece. Then she sought Ruth in haste.

Ruth had just gone upstairs. Erskine was surprised to see her back in his study almost immediately, and startled by her mode of entrance, which suggested sudden illness in the house.

"What in the world has happened?" he said, sitting upright in his chair.

"Happened?" cried Ruth bitterly. "It is the last straw! I give her up. I wash my hands of her. I wish she had never come over!"

"Tiny? Why, what has she been doing now?"

"It isn't what she has been doing—it is what she says she's going to do. You may be able to bring her to reason, but I never shall. I won't try—I wash my hands of her. I will say no more to her. But it is simply disgraceful! She is far worse than Herbert!"

"Has she unmade her mind," Holland asked eagerly.

"No, no, no! But worse, I call it. O Erskine, if you knew what she says——"

"I am waiting to hear."

"You'll never guess!"

"No, I give it up."

"So must Tiny—I never heard a madder idea in my life!"

"Than *what*, my dear?"

"Her going out with Herbert in the *Ballaarat*!"

CHAPTER XVIII.
THE THIRD TIME OF ASKING.

December was at hand soon enough, and with the month came Lord Manister for his answer. Though more than slightly nervous he entered the modest house in Kensington with his head very high; and certain inappropriate sensations visited him during the few minutes he was kept waiting in the drawing room. He did not sit down. Then it was Tiny Luttrell who opened the door, and those sensations made good their escape from a bosom in which they had no business. In the living presence of the person one proposes to marry there are some misgivings that had need be impossible—Christina little suspected her privilege of shutting the door on Manister's with her own hand. He sat down at her example.

But if he was nervous so was she, and as he came bravely to the point she found it more and more difficult to meet his hungry eyes. It was rather rare for Christina to experience any difficulty of the kind. She rose, and stood in front of the fire, with her back to the room and Lord Manister. There, with her forehead resting on the rim of the mantelpiece (for Tiny that was not far to bend), and while the hot fire scorched her plain gray skirt and gave a needed color to the downcast face, she heard what Manister had to say. Soon she knew that he was saying it with his elbow on one end of the mantelpiece; and liked him for facing her so, and compelling her to face him. But when she found him waiting for his answer, she gave him it without lifting her eyes from the fire.

"No!"

He had asked her whether she had been able to make up her mind. The answer she had given was, indeed, the truth; but it had been prepared for a more conclusive question. She was vexed with him for the question he had chosen to put first; and the more so because it had snatched from her an admission which she had not intended to make. But she had not made up her mind—that was the simple truth; and now she trusted that he would make up his.

Instead of which he said sadly, after a pause:

"I wanted to give you six months!"

"It was very wrong of you to give me one," she answered with startling ingratitude.

"Why wrong?"

"You might have seen that I was unworthy of you."

"I might have given up loving you, I suppose, in a second!"

"I wish you would——"

"I never shall!"

"If you ever began," Christina added to her own sentence. At last her face was raised, and now it was his eyes that fell before the cool acumen of her smile.

"You don't believe in me yet!" he groaned. "Not yet, though I wait, wait, wait."

"No one asked you to wait," Lord Manister was reminded.

"But you see that I can't help it! You see that I am miserable about you!"

This indeed was sufficiently plain; and the sight of his misery was softening Christina by degrees. She said more kindly:

"Listen to me, Lord Manister. It is a month since you saw me. At this moment you may feel what you are saying. Very well, then, you *do* feel it; but have you felt it throughout the last month? Have you felt so patient—you are far too patient—all the time? Has it never seemed to you that my keeping you in doubt, even for one month, was a piece of impertinence you ought never to have stood? Wouldn't your friends simply think you mad if they knew how you were allowing me to use you? Haven't you yourself occasionally remembered who you are, and who I am, and burst out laughing? I must say I have; it sometimes seems to me so utterly absurd—— And you see you can't answer my questions!"

He could not; one after another they had penetrated to the quick.

"They are not fair questions," Manister said doggedly. "What may have crossed my mind when I have felt worried and wretched has nothing to do with it. Isn't it enough that I tell you I can wait your own good time—that I feel a pride in waiting, now we are together and I am looking in your eyes?"

"No, I don't think that's quite enough," replied Christina softly. "It would hardly be enough, you know, if you only felt me worth waiting for while you were with me. That would mean that for some reason I fascinated you. And fascination isn't love, Lord Manister. I don't want to be rude—much less unkind—but I can't believe that you have ever been really in love with me; I simply can't!"

Yet she had never felt so near to that belief before. Her words, however, helped Lord Manister back to his dignity.

"Of course you must believe only what you choose," said he loftily. "One cannot force you to believe in one's sincerity. I suppose I spoilt you for believing in mine some time since. At all events you were fond of me once!

Only a month ago you liked me all but well enough to marry me. Yet now you do not know!"

"Therefore the decision is left to you, Lord Manister; you must give me up."

"Never! while you are free."

His teeth were clenched.

"But do consider. Most probably I shall never care enough for you to marry you. And oh! I wonder how you can look at me when no other girl in the world would refuse you!"

"Can't you see that this is part of your charm?" cried the young man impulsively. "You are the one girl I know who is not worldly. You are the one girl I want!"

Christina shook her head.

"If I have any charm at all, you oughtn't to know what it is—you ought to love me you can't say why—there's no sizing up real love!" she informed him rapidly, but with a smile. "There's another thing, too. You cannot be used to being treated as I have treated you in many ways. I have often been intensely rude to you. I can't help thinking there must be a good deal of pique in your feeling toward me."

"There is more real love," returned Manister, "if I know it!"

"I wonder if you do know it?" said the girl, with a laugh; but she was wondering very seriously in her heart. He protested no more; she liked him for that, too, as also for the briskness in his tone and manner when he spoke next.

"You say you don't care for me enough, and you say I don't care for you properly, and we won't argue any more about either matter for the moment." He had flung back his head from the hand that had shaded his eyes; his elbow remained on the chimney-piece, but now he was standing erect. "There is something else," said Lord Manister, "that has prevented you from coming to a decision."

"There is certainly one thing that has had something to do with it."

"May I ask what it is?"

"Certainly, Lord Manister. I am going back to Australia."

"Soon?" This was after a pause, during which their eyes had not met.

"Sooner than was intended."

"Is it—is it for any special reason that—that you have kept from me?"

He was agitated by a sudden thought, which she read. She shook her head reassuringly.

"No, it is not to get married, nor yet engaged."

"Then there is no one out there?"

"There is no one anywhere that I could marry for love. That's the simple truth. I am going back to Australia because Herbert is going. Cambridge doesn't suit him, and I'm sorry to say he doesn't suit Cambridge. We came over together, so we are going back together. That, I promise you, is the whole and only explanation. I myself did not want to go so soon."

"But surely you are not going this year?"

"We are—before Christmas."

As Tiny spoke her glance went to the window: she was very anxious to see the snow before she sailed, but none had fallen yet, though December had come in dull and raw.

"But your people here must be very much against that?"

"They were, but now it is settled."

"You must have promised to come back!"

Christina seemed surprised.

"Yes, I said I would come back some day."

"And you shall!" cried Manister passionately. "You shall come back as my wife! Do you suppose I am going to stop short at this, when but for your brother you would have been mine to-day? I don't mean to say he has influenced you, except by going back so soon; you love Australia, and you must needs go back with him. Then go! I told you to take six months; you have taken one of them. When the other five are up I am coming to you again wherever you may be. Till then I will take no answer; and whatever it may be in the end I bow to it—I bow to it!"

His passion surprised and even moved Christina; but his humility stirred up in her soul a contempt which mingled strangely with her pity. Women of spirit cannot admire the man who will submit to anything at their hands. Christina would willingly have given admiration in exchange for the love in which she was beginning to believe; it would have pleased her sense of justice, it would have promoted her self-respect to make some such small payment on account. With Manister's patience she had none at all. She was disappointed in him. Her foot tapped angrily on the fender.

"But I don't want you to wait!" exclaimed Christina ungraciously. "I have told you so already."

"Still I mean to do so, and it serves me right."

This touched her generosity.

"Ah, don't say that!" she cried earnestly. "Oh, Lord Manister, I have forgotten all old scores—I never think of them now! The balance has been the other way so long; and I do not deserve another chance."

"Ah, but Tiny—darling—it is I who am asking for that!"

His tone compelled her to meet his gaze—its intensity made her wince.

"You believe in me!" he cried joyously. "Say only that you believe in me, and I will go away now. I will go away happy and proud—to wait—for you."

Then Tiny laid her little hand on his arm, and her eyes that had filled with tears answered him to his present satisfaction. He held her hand for just a few seconds before he went, and in kindness she returned his pressure. Then the shutting of the front door down below made her realize that he was gone. And she had time to dry her eyes and to gather herself together before Ruth, whose hopes had been dead some days, came into the room with a dejected mien and pointedly abstained from asking questions.

"If it interests you to hear it," Tiny said lightly, "I am converted to your creed at last; I believe in Lord Manister!"

"But you are not engaged to him," Ruth said wearily; "I see you are not."

"I am not; but he insists on waiting. If only he wasn't so tame! But I can't help believing in him now; and that settles it."

"Nothing is settled until you are engaged," said the matter-of-fact sister, with a sigh.

"Nevertheless I'm going to try with all my might to care for him, now that I see that he must really care for me. And let me tell you that I shall consider myself all the more bound to him because I haven't *said* yes, and because we're *not* actually engaged!"

"Yes?" said the other incredulously. "That is so like you, Tiny!"

And Ruth almost sneered.

CHAPTER XIX.
COUNSEL'S OPINION.

The worst of it all was this: that the young man himself had not invariably that confidence in his own affections which displayed itself so bravely and so convincingly at a psychological moment. Not that Manister was insincere, exactly. If you come to think of it, you may deceive others with perfect innocence, having once deceived yourself. And this was exactly what had happened.

There was one distinctive feature of the case: away from Christina Luttrell the poor fellow had already had his doubts of himself; in her presence those doubts were as certain to evaporate as snowflakes in the warmth of the sun.

Even as he went down Mrs. Holland's stairs Manister was joined by certain invisible companions—the misgivings that had made their escape as Christina entered the room. They had waited for him on the landing outside the door. They led and followed him downstairs. They linked arms with him in the street. They stifled him in his hansom, which they boarded ruthlessly. In one of the silent rooms of the club to which he drove they talked to him silently, sitting on the arms of his saddle-back chair and arguing all at once. Powerless to shake them off he was forced to bear with them, to hear what they had to say, to answer them where he could.

Mingling with the importunate voices of his inner consciousness were the remembered words of the girl. She had asked him whether he had never burst out laughing as the affair presented itself in certain lights; he did so now, silently, it is true, but with exceeding bitterness. She had told him that it was not enough that he should feel willing to wait for her when they were together; and now that he had left her, though so lately, he was certainly less inclined to be patient. She had suggested that he was more fascinated than in love; and already he knew that her suggestion had given shape and utterance to a vague suspicion of his own soul. She had gone so far as to hint at the possible secret of his infatuation, and there again she had hit the mark; though apart from her talent of torture her sweet looks and charming ways had been strong wine to Manister from the first. Still her snubs had piqued his passion in the beginning of things out in Melbourne; and here in Europe she had virtually refused him three times. Modest he might be, and yet know that this were a rare experience for such as himself at the hands of such as Tiny Luttrell. On the whole, the experience was sufficiently complete as it stood; yet he could not help wishing to win; indeed, he had gone too far to draw back, and for that reason alone the idea of defeat in the end was intolerable to him. And this was the one spring of his actions which seemed to have escaped Christina's notice; the others she had detected with an acuteness which made him wonder, for the first time, whether on her very merits she would be a comfortable person to live with, after all.

Gradually, however, these echoes of the late interview grew fainter in his ears, and its upshot came home to Manister with sensations of chagrin sharper than any he had endured in all his life before. His feelings when refused by this girl in the previous August, and under peculiarly humiliating circumstances, were enviable compared with his feelings now. Then he had deserved his humiliation—at least he was generous enough to say so—and he had taken what he called his punishment in a very manly spirit. But the desire to win had sent him on a secret mission to Cintra, on the chance of seeing her there, and his present feelings reminded him of those with which he had beaten his retreat from Portugal. For he had gone there for a final answer, and had come back without one; and to-day he had suffered afresh that selfsame humiliation, only in an aggravated form, and more voluntarily than ever. She had never asked him to wait; he had offered on both occasions to wait six months—nay, he had insisted on waiting. Even now, within a couple of hours after the event, he could scarcely credit his own weakness and stultification. He was by no means so weak in affairs wherein the affections played no part. He firmly believed that no other woman could have twisted him round her finger as this one had done. But here, perhaps, we have merely the everyday spectacle of a young man discerning exceptional excuses for a realized infirmity; and the point is that Manister realized his weakness this evening as he had never done before. The girl herself had made him look inward. She had suggested fascination, not love. That suggestion stuck painfully. Yet he was not sure.

Never had he felt so horribly unsure of himself; in the midst of his self-distrust there came to him, suddenly, the recollection that she distrusted him no longer, and there was actually some comfort in this thought, which is strange when you note its fellows, but due less to the contradictoriness of human nature than to the supremacy of a young man's vanity. He stood well with her now. She believed in him at last. Propped up by these reflections, he began almost to believe in himself. At least a momentary complacency was the result.

The improvement in his spirits allowed Lord Manister to give heed to another portion of his organism which had for some time been inviting him to go into another room and dine. Now he did so, with a sharp eye for acquaintances, whom he had no desire to meet. For this reason he had driven to the club which he had joined most recently; it was not a young man's club, so he felt fairly safe from his friends. Yet he had hardly ordered his soup, and was searching the wine list for the choice brand which the circumstances seemed to demand, when a heavy hand dropped upon his shoulder, and his glance leapt from the wine list to the last face he expected or wished to see—that of his kinsman Captain Dromard.

Captain Dromard was a cousin of the present earl, and notoriously the rolling stone of his house. Manister had seen him last in Melbourne, and ever since had borne him a grudge which he was not likely to forget. Had he dreamt that the captain (who had been last heard of in Borneo) was in London, Manister would have shunned this club in order to avoid the risk of meeting him; but it seemed that Captain Dromard had landed in England only that morning: and they dined together, of course; and Manister made the best of it. His kinsman was a big, grizzled, florid man, with an imperial, and with a comic wicked cut about him which made one laugh. But he retained an unpleasant trick of treating Manister as a mere boy: for instance, he was in time to choose the brand, and, as he said before the waiter, to prevent Manister from poisoning himself. He was, however, an entertaining person, and at his best to-night, being wont to delight in London for a day or two before realizing the infernal qualities of the climate and arranging fresh travels. But Manister was not entertained; he tried to appear so, but the captain saw through the pretense, and immediately scented a woman. There were reasons why the rolling stone was particularly good at detecting this element—which always interested him. His interest was unusual in the present instance, owing to certain reminiscences of Manister in Melbourne during his own flying visit to that port. It was during a subsequent week-end in England that Captain Dromard had alarmed the countess, with a result of which he was as yet unaware; but he did not hesitate to make inquiries now, and he began by asking Manister how he had managed to get out of the scrape in which he had left him.

"I remember no scrape," said Manister stiffly.

"You don't? Well, perhaps I put it too strongly," conceded the captain. "We'll say no more about it, my boy. Devilish pretty little thing, though; remember her well, but could never recall her name. By the bye, I'm afraid I terrified your mother over that; feared she was going to cable you home next day; was sorry I spoke."

"So was I," Manister said dryly, but, by an effort, not forbiddingly, so that the captain saw no harm in raising his glass.

"Well, here's to the lady's health, my boy, whoever she was, and wherever she may be!"

Manister smiled across his glass and drained it in silence. There was a glitter in his young eyes which made it difficult for the captain to drop the subject finally. Manister had been drinking freely, without becoming flushed, which is another sign of trouble. The captain could not help saying confidentially:

"You know, Harry, your mother was so keen for you to marry one of old Acklam's daughters. That's what frightened her. But it is to come off some day, isn't it?"

"Can't say," said Lord Manister.

"It ought to, Harry. I like to see a young fellow with your position marry properly, and settle down. I don't know which of the Garths it is, but I've always heard one of 'em was the girl you liked."

"Suppose the girl you like won't marry you?" Manister exclaimed, with a sudden change of manner, and in the tone of one consulting an authority.

"Well, there's an end on't."

"Ah, but suppose she can't make up her mind?"

"You might give her a month—though I wouldn't."

"Suppose a month is not enough for her?"

The captain stared; his bronzed forehead became barred with furrows; his eyes turned stony with indignation.

"A month not enough for her to make up her mind—about you?" he said at length incredulously. "Good God, sir, see her to the devil!"

Then Lord Manister showed his teeth. Though he had consulted the captain, he took his advice badly. He said you could not be much in love to be choked off so easily; he hinted that his kinsman had never been much in love. Captain Dromard intimated in reply that whether that was the case or not he was not without experience of a sort, and he could tell Harry that no woman under heaven was worth kneeling in the mud to, which Harry said hotly was unnecessary information. So they went elsewhere to smoke, and later on to a music hall, the subject having been left for good in the club coffee room. The following afternoon, however, Lord Manister drove through the snow with a very resolute front to show to Tiny Luttrell, who was just then passing Deal in the *Ballaarat*, without having given him the faintest notion yesterday that she was to sail to-day.

CHAPTER XX.
IN HONOR BOUND.

Aboard the *Ballaarat* Christina committed a new eccentricity, but it may be well to state at once, a perfectly harmless one. She confided in another girl—a practice which Tiny had avoided all her life. And this very girl had offended her at first sight by looking aggressively happy when the boat sailed and all nice women were in tears.

There had been a time when Christina seldom cried, but in England she had grown very soft in some ways, and she looked her last at it, and at the snow that had fallen in the night as if to please her, through blinding tears. She had never in her life felt more acutely wretched than when saying good-by to Ruth and Erskine, and her sorrow was heightened by the feeling that she had been both unkind and ungrateful to Ruth, to whom she clung for forgiveness at the last moment. The reason why her parting words were jocular, though broken, was because the sight of an honest, smiling face, which might have blushed for smiling then, sent a fleam of irritation through her heart that awoke the latent mischief in her wet eyes.

"I do wish you would ask Erskine to throw a snowball at that depressing person," she whispered to Ruth, "who does nothing but laugh and look really happy! If it was only put on for the sake of her friends I could forgive her; but it isn't. Tell him I mean it—there's no fun in me to-day; and you may also tell him that it would have been only brotherly of him to kiss me on this occasion, when we may all be going to the bottom!"

Erskine, who had crossed the gangway before his wife, so that she need not feel that he overheard her final words to her own kin, shook his head at Tiny when Ruth joined him on the quay. But his smile was lifeless; there was no fun in him either to-day. He drew his wife's arm through his own, and Tiny saw the last of them standing together thus. They stood in snow and mud, but the railway shed behind them was a great sheet of unsullied whiteness, softly edging the bright December sky, and Christina never forgot her first glimpse of the snow and her last of Ruth and Erskine. When their figures were gone and only the snow was left for Christina's eyes, they filled afresh, and she broke hastily from Herbert, who was himself uncommonly dejected. She hurried unsteadily to her cabin, to find her cabin companion singing softly to herself as she unstrapped her rugs; for her cabin companion was, of course, the odiously cheerful person who already on deck had done violence to Christina's feelings.

Thus the acquaintance began in a particularly unpromising manner; but the cheerful person turned out to be as bad a sailor as Christina was a good one, and she met with much practical kindness at Christina's hands, which had a clever, tender way with them, though in other respects the good sailor was not from the first so sympathetic. It is harder than it ought to be to sympathize with the seasick when one is quite well one's self; still Christina found it impossible not to admire her extraordinary companion, who kept up her spirits during a whole week spent in her berth, and was more cheerful than ever at the end of it, when she could scarcely stand. Then Christina expressed her admiration, likewise her curiosity, and received a simple explanation. The cheerful person was on her way to Colombo and the altar-rails. Her *trousseau* was in the hold.

The two became exceeding fast friends, and their friendship was founded on mutual envy. Tiny was envied for the various qualities which made her greatly admired on board, for that admiration itself, and for the marked manner in which she paid no heed to it; and she envied her friend a very ordinary love story, now approaching a very ordinary end. The cheerful girl was plain, unaccomplished, and not at all young. But there was one whom she loved better than herself; she was properly engaged; she was happy in her engagement; her soul was settled and at peace. Also she was good, and Christina envied her far more than she envied Christina, who would listen wistfully to the commonplace expression of a commonplace happiness, but was herself much more reserved. It was only when the other girl guessed it that she admitted that she also was "as good as engaged." The other girl clamored to know all about it; and ultimately, in the Indian Ocean, she discovered that Christina was not the least in love with the man to whom she was as good as engaged. Then this honest person spoke her mind with extreme freedom, and Christina, instead of being offended, opened her own heart as freely, merely keeping to herself the man's name and never hinting at his high degree. She declared that she was morally bound to him, adding that she had treated him badly enough already; her friend ridiculed the bond, and told her how she would be treating him worse than ever. Christina argued—it was curious how fond she was of arguing the matter, and how she allowed herself to be lectured by a stranger. But these two were not strangers now; the cheerful girl was the best friend Tiny had ever made among women. They parted with a wrench at Colombo, where Tiny saw the other safely into the arms of a gentleman of a suitably happy and ordinary appearance; and so one more friend passed in and out of the young girl's life, leaving a deeper mark in the three weeks than either of them suspected.

The rest of the voyage dragged terribly with Christina, which is an unusual experience for the prettiest girl aboard an Australian liner; only on this voyage the prettiest girl was also the most unsociable. Beyond her late companion (whose berth remained empty to depress Christina whenever she entered the cabin) Miss Luttrell had formed few acquaintances and no friendships between London and Colombo; between Colombo and Melbourne she simply preyed upon herself. Herbert remonstrated with her, and the third officer—who had been fourth on the boat in which they had come over—was excessively interested, remembering the difference six months earlier. Then, indeed, Christina had found a good deal to say to all the officers, including the captain, whom she had chaffed notoriously; but now she would stay out late and alone on the starlit deck without ever breaking the rules by conversing with the officer of the watch (her pet trick formerly), and only the third, who knew her of old, had the right to bid her good-day. Tiny's cheerful friend had left her wretched and apprehensive. She saw the Southern Cross rise out of the Southern Sea without a thrill of welcome, but rather with a vague dismay; from the after-rail she said good-by to the Great Bear with a shudder at the thought of seeing it again. Neither end of the earth presented a very peaceful prospect to Christina as she hovered between the two on the steamer's deck. She had quite made up her mind to return to England, however, and to reward Lord Manister's long-suffering docility by marrying him at the end of the six months. Meanwhile she would enjoy Australia and tell only one of her friends there. One she must tell, and with her own lips, in case she should be misjudged. And thinking not a little of her own justification, she invented a small sophistry with which to defend herself as occasion might arise. She argued that two men were in love with her, that she herself was in love with neither, but that she liked one of them too well to marry him without love. Therefore, she said, the easiest way out of it was to marry the other, who not only had less in him to satisfy, but who had more to give in place of real happiness. She was proud of this argument. She was sorry it had not occurred to her before stopping at Colombo—forgetting that she had told her friend of only one man who was in love with her. But the heart starves on sophistry with nothing to it; and with Christina the voyage dragged cruelly to its end.

But the moment she landed in Melbourne a good thing happened to her—she was snatched out of herself. A common shock and anxiety awaited both Christina and Herbert Luttrell: they found their mother in tears over a piece of very bad news from Wallandoon. It seemed that Mr. Luttrell had gone up to the station the week before to choose the site for a well which he was about to sink at considerable expense, and that he was now lying at the old homestead with a broken leg, the result of a buggy accident with a pair of young horses. He was able to write with his own hand in pencil, and he mentioned that Swift had fetched a surgeon from the river in the quickest time ever known; that the surgeon had set the leg quite successfully, so that there was no occasion for anxiety, though naturally he should be unable to leave Wallandoon for some weeks. He expressed forcibly the hope that his wife would not think of joining him there; she was not strong enough, and he needed no attention. Nevertheless, had the *Ballaarat* arrived one day later, Mrs. Luttrell would have gone. Her two children were in time to restrain her, but only by undertaking to go instead. Before they could realize that they had spent an afternoon and a night in Melbourne they had left the city and had embarked on an inland voyage of five hundred miles up country.

So their first full day ashore was spent in a railway carriage; but all that night the stars were in their eyes, and the gum trees racing by on either hand, and the warm wind fanning their faces, because Tiny would never travel inside the coach. They were back in Riverina. The Murray coiled behind them; the Murrumbidgee lay before. And the night after that they were creeping across the desert of the One Tree Plain, with the Lachlan lying ahead and the Murrumbidgee left behind. Here the leather-hung coach labored in the mud, for the Lachlan district was suffering before it could profit from a rather heavy rainfall three days old; and the driver flogged seven horses all night long instead of mildly chastening five, and the girl at his side could not have slept if she had tried, but she did not try. To her the night seemed too good to miss. The stars shone brilliantly from rim to rim of the unbroken plain, and upward from the overflowing crab-holes, and even in the flooded ruts, where the coach wheels split and scattered them like quicksilver beneath the thumb. There was no conversation on the coach. On the eve of facing his father Herbert was rehearsing his defense, while Tiny was just reveling in the night, and feeling very happy, so she said.

For a couple of hours before dawn they rested at Booligal. But Booligal is notorious for its mosquitoes, and there had been three inches of rain there, so the rest was a mockery. Tiny had a bed to lie down on, but she did not lie long. She was found by Herbert (who smoked six pipes in those two hours), leaning against one of the veranda posts as if asleep on her feet, but with eyes fixed intently upon a dull, reddening arc on the very edge of the darkling plain.

"By the time we get there," said Herbert severely, "you'll be just about dished! What on earth are you doing out here instead of taking a spell when you can get it?"

"I'm watching for the sun," murmured Christina, without moving. "It's a regular Australian dawn; you never saw one like it in England. Here the sun gets up in the middle of the night, and there he very often doesn't get up at all. Oh, but it's glorious to be back—don't *you* think so, old Herbs?"

"I might—if it wasn't for the governor."

Tiny flushed with shame. She had forgotten the accident. Being reminded of it she turned her back on the sunrise in deep contrition, but she had not taken Herbert's meaning.

"I funk facing him," said he gloomily. "I have nothing to say for myself, and if I had a fellow couldn't say it with the poor governor lying on his back."

"Poor old Herbs!" said Tiny kindly. "I don't think you have much to fear, however. It was our mistake in wanting you to go to Cambridge when you'd been your own boss always. You were born for the bush—I'm not sure that we both weren't!"

He did not hear her sigh.

"It's all very well for you to talk, Tiny! You haven't to make your peace with anybody—you haven't to confess that you've made a ghastly fool of yourself!"

"Have I not?" exclaimed the girl bitterly.

"I thought you weren't going to mention his name?" Herbert said in surprise.

"No more I am," replied Tiny, recovering herself. "So, as you say, it is all very well for me to talk." And as she turned a ball of fire was balanced on the distant rim of the plain, and the arc above was now a semicircle of crimson, which blended even yet with the lingering shades of night.

Even Herbert was not in all Tiny's secrets. He never dreamt that she had before her an ordeal far worse than his own. When they sighted the little township where the station buggy always met the coach, he thought her excitement due to obvious and natural causes. The township roofs gleamed in the afternoon sun for half an hour before one could distinguish even a looked-for object, such as a buggy drawn up in the shade at the hotel veranda. Herbert had time to become excited himself, in spite of the ignoble circumstances of his return.

"I see it!" he exclaimed with confidence, at five hundred yards. "And good old Bushman and Brownlock are the pair. I'd spot 'em a mile off."

"Can you see who it is in the buggy?" asked Tiny, at two hundred. She was sitting like a mouse between Herbert and the driver.

"I shall in a shake; I think it's Jack Swift."

He did not know how her heart was beating. At fifty yards he said, "It isn't Swift; it's one of the hands. I've never seen this joker before."

"Ah!" said Tiny, and that was all. Herbert had no ear for a tone.

CHAPTER XXI.
A DEAF EAR.

The manager of Wallandoon was harder at work that afternoon than any man on the run. This was generally the case when there was hard work to be done; when there was not, however, Swift had a way of making work for himself. He had made his work to-day. Nothing need have prevented his meeting the coach himself; but it had occurred to Swift that he would be somewhat in the way at the meeting between Mr. Luttrell and his children, while with regard to his own meeting with Christina he felt much nervousness, which night, perhaps, would partly cloak. This, however, was an instinct rather than a motive. Instinctively also he sought by violent labor to expel the fever from his mind. He was absurdly excited, and his energy during the heat of the day was little less than insane. So at any rate it seemed to the youth who was helping him by looking on, while Swift covered in half a tank with brushwood. The tank had been almost dry, but was newly filled by the rains, and the partial covering was designed to delay evaporation. But Swift himself would execute his own design, and thought nothing of standing up to his chest in the water, clothed only in his wide-awake, though he was the manager of the station. The young storekeeper did not admire him for it, though he could not help envying the manager his thick arms, which were also bronzed, like the manager's face and neck, and in striking contrast to the whiteness of his deep chest and broad shoulders. There had been a change in storekeepers during recent months, a change not by any means for the better.

Near the tank were some brushwood yards, which were certainly in need of repairs, but the need was far from immediate. Swift, however, chose to mend up the fences that night, while he happened to be on the spot, and his young assistant had no choice but to watch him. It was dark when at last they rode back together to the station, silent, hungry, and not pleased with one another; for Swift was one of those energetic people whom it is difficult to help unless you are energetic yourself; and the new storekeeper was not. This youth did little for his rations that day until the homestead was reached. Then the manager left him to unsaddle and feed both horses, and himself walked over to the veranda, whence came the sound of voices.

Mr. Luttrell was lying in the long deck chair which had been procured from a neighboring station, and Herbert was smoking demurely at his side. Christina was not there at all.

"You will find her in the dining room," Mr. Luttrell said, as his son and the manager shook hands. "She has gone to make tea for you; she means to look after us all for the next few weeks."

The dining room was at the back of the house, and as Swift walked round to it he stepped from the veranda into the heavy sand in which the homestead was planted. He could not help it. His love had grown upon him since that short week with her, nine months before. He felt that if his eyes rested upon her first he could take her hand more steadily. So he stood and watched her a moment as she bent over the tea table with lowered head and busy fingers, and there was something so like his dreams in the sight of her there that he almost cried out aloud. Next instant his spurs jingled in the veranda. She raised her head with a jerk; he saw the fear of himself in her eyes—and knew.

It did not blind him to her haggard looks.

When they had shaken hands he could not help saying, "It is evident that the old country doesn't agree with you, as you feared." And when it was too late he would have altered the remark.

"Seeing that it's six weeks since I left it, and that I have been traveling night and day since I landed, you are rather hard on the old country."

So she answered him, her fingers in the tea caddy, and her eyes with them. The lamplight shone upon her freckles as Swift studied her anxiously. Perhaps, as she hinted, she was only tired.

"I say, I can't have you making tea for me!" Swift exclaimed nervously. "You are worn out, and I am accustomed to doing all this sort of thing for myself."

"Then you will have the kindness to unaccustom yourself! I am mistress here until papa is fit to be moved."

And not a day longer. He knew it by the way she avoided his eyes. Yet he was forced to make conversation.

"Why do you warm the teapot?"

"It is the proper thing to do."

"I never knew that!"

"I dare say it isn't the only thing you never knew. I shouldn't wonder if you swallowed your coffee with cold milk?"

"Of course we do—when we have coffee."

"Ah, it is good for you to have a housekeeper for a time," said Christina cruelly, she did not know why.

"It's my firm belief," remarked Swift, "that you have learnt these dodges in England, and that you did *not* detest the whole thing!"

The words had a far-away familiar sound to Christina, and they were spoken in the pointed accents with which one quotes.

"Did I say I should detest the whole thing?" asked Christina, marking the tablecloth with a fork.

"You did; they were your very words."

"Come, I don't believe that."

"I can't help it; those were your words. They were your very last words to me."

"And you actually remember them?"

She looked at him, smiling; but his face put out her smile, and the wave of compassion which now swept over hers confirmed the knowledge that had come to him with her first frightened glance.

The storekeeper, who came in before more was said, was the unconscious witness of a well-acted interlude of which he was also the cause. He approved of Miss Luttrell at the tea tray, and was to some extent recompensed for the hard day's work he had not done. He left her with Swift on the back veranda, and they might have been grateful to him, for not only had his advent been a boon to them both at a very awkward moment, but, in going, he supplied them with a topic.

"What has happened to my little Englishman?" Christina asked at once. "I hoped to find him here still."

"I wish you had. He was a fine fellow, and this one is not."

"Then you didn't mean to get rid of my little friend?"

"No. It's a very pretty story," Swift said slowly, as he watched her in the starlight. "His father died, and he went home and came in for something; and now that little chap is actually married to the girl he used to talk about!"

Tiny was silent for some moments. Then she laughed.

"So much for my advice! His case is the exception that proves my rule."

"I happen to remember your advice. So you still think the same?"

"Most certainly I do."

He laughed sardonically. "You might just as well tell me outright that you are engaged to be married."

The girl recoiled.

"How do you know?" she cried. "Who has told you?"

"You have—now. Your eyes told me twenty minutes ago."

"But it isn't true! Nobody knows anything about it! It isn't a real engagement yet!"

"I have no doubt it will be real enough for me," answered Swift very bitterly; and he moved away from her, though her little hands were stretched out to keep him.

"Don't leave me!" she cried piteously. "I want to tell you. I will tell you now, if you will only let me."

He faced about, with one foot on the veranda and the other in the sand.

"Tell me," he said, "if it is that old affair come right; that is all I care to know."

"It is; but it hasn't come right yet—perhaps it never will. If only you would let me tell you everything!"

"Thank you; I dare say I can imagine how matters stand. I think I told you it would all come right. I am very glad it has."

"Jack!"

But Jack was gone. In the starlight she watched him disappear among the pines. He walked so slowly that she fancied him whistling, and would have given very much for some such sign of outward indifference to show that he cared; but no sound came to her save the chirrup of the crickets, which never ceased in the night time at Wallandoon. And that made her listen for the champing of the solitary animal in the horse yard, until she heard it, too, and stood still to listen to both noises of the night. She remembered how once or twice in England she had seemed to hear these two sounds, and how she had longed to be back again in the old veranda. Now she was back. This was the old, old veranda. And those two old sounds were beating into her brain in very reality—without pause or pity.

"Why, Tiny," said Herbert later, "this is the second time to-day! I believe you *can* sleep on end like a blooming native-companion. You're to come and talk to the governor; he would like you to sit with him before we carry him into his room."

"Would he?" Tiny cried out, and a moment later she was kneeling by the deck chair and sobbing wildly on her father's breast.

"Just because I told her she'd dish herself," remarked Herbert, looking on with irritation, "she's been and gone and done it. That's still her line!"

CHAPTER XXII.
SUMMUM BONUM.

For a month Christina declined to leave her father's side, much against his will, but the girl's will was stronger. She was as though tethered to the long deck chair until the lame man became able to leave it on two sticks. Then she flew to the other extreme.

North of the Lachlan the recent rains had been less heavy than in Lower Riverina. On Wallandoon less than two inches had fallen, and by February it was found necessary to resume work at the eight-mile whim. But the whim driver had gone off with his check when the rain gave him a holiday, and he had never returned. There was a momentary difficulty in finding a man to replace him, and it was then that Miss Tiny startled the station by herself volunteering for the post. At first Mr. Luttrell would not hear of the plan, but the manager's opinion was not asked, and he carefully refrained from giving it, while Herbert (who was about to be intrusted with a mob of wethers for the Melbourne market) took his sister's side. He pointed out with truth that any fool could drive a whim under ordinary circumstances, and that, as Tiny would hardly petition to sleep at the whim, the long ride morning and evening would do her no harm. Mr. Luttrell gave in then. He had tried in vain to drive the young girl from his side. She had watched over him with increasing solicitude, with an almost unnatural tenderness. She had shown him a warmer heart than heretofore he had known her to possess, and an amount of love and affection which he felt to be more than a father's share. He did not know what was the matter, but he made guesses. It had been his lifelong practice not to "interfere" with his children; hence the earliest misdeeds of his daughter Tiny; hence, also, the academic career of his son Herbert. Mr. Luttrell put no questions to the girl, and none concerning her to her brother, which was nice of him, seeing that her ways had made him privately inquisitive; but he took Herbert's advice and let Christina drive the eight-mile whim.

The experiment proved a complete success, but then plain whim driving is not difficult. Christina spent an hour or so two or three times a day in driving the whim horse round and round until the tank was full, after which it was no trouble to keep the troughs properly supplied. The rest of her time she occupied in reading or musing in the shadow of the tank; but each day she boiled her "billy" in the hut, eating very heartily in her seclusion, and delighting more and more in the temporary freedom of her existence, as a boy in holidays that are drawing to an end. The whim stood high on a plain, the wind whistled through its timbers, and each evening the girl brought back to the homestead a higher color and a lighter step. In these days, however, very little was seen of her. She would come in tired, and soon secrete herself within four newspapered walls; and she went out of her way to discourage visitors at the whim. Of this she made such a point that the manager, on coming in earlier than usual one afternoon, was surprised when Herbert, whom he met riding out from the station, informed him that he was on his way to the eight-mile to look up the whim driver. Herbert seemed to have something on his mind, and presently he told Swift what it was. He had awkward news for Tiny, which he had decided to tell her at once and be done with it. But he did not like the job. He liked it so little that he went the length of confiding in Swift as to the nature of the news. The manager annoyed him—he had not a remark to make.

Herbert rode moodily on his way. He was sorry that he had spoken to Swift (whose stolid demeanor was a surprise to him, as well as an irritation); he had undoubtedly spoken too freely. With Swift still in his thoughts, Luttrell was within a mile of the whim, and cantering gently, before he became aware that another rider was overtaking him at a gallop; and as he turned in his saddle, the manager himself bore down upon him with a strange look in his good eyes.

"I want you to let me—tell Tiny!" Jack Swift said hoarsely, as Herbert stared. Jack's was a look of pure appeal.

"You?"

"Yes——You understand?"

"That's all right! I thought I couldn't have been mistaken," said Herbert, still looking him in the eyes. "By ghost, Jack, you're a sportsman!"

He held out his hand, and Swift gripped it. In another minute they were a quarter of a mile apart; but it was Swift who was riding on to the whim, very slowly now, and with his eyes on the black timbers rising clear of the sand against the sky. He could never look at them without hearing words and tones that it was still bitter to remember; and now he was going—to break bad news to Tiny? That was his undertaking.

He found the whim driver with her book in the shadow of the tank.

"Good-afternoon," Christina said very civilly, though her eyebrows had arched at the sight of him. "Have you come to see whether the troughs are full, or am I wanted at the homestead?"

"Neither," said Swift, smiling; "only the mail is in, and there are letters from England."

"How good of you!" exclaimed the girl, holding out her hand.

Swift was embarrassed.

"Now you will pitch into me! I haven't seen the letters, and I don't know whether there is one for you: but I met Herbert, and he told me he had heard from your sister; and—and I thought you might like to hear that, as I was coming this way."

"It is still good of you," said Christina kindly; and that made him honest.

"It isn't a bit good, because I came this way to speak to you about something else."

"Really?"

"Yes, because one sees so little of you now, and soon you will be going. The truth is something has been rankling with me ever since the night you arrived—nothing you said to me; it was my own behavior to you——"

"Which wasn't pretty," interrupted Tiny.

"I know it wasn't; I have been very sorry for it. When you offered to tell me about your engagement I wouldn't listen. I would listen now!"

"And now I shouldn't dream of telling you a word," Tiny said, staring coolly in his face; "not even if I *were* engaged."

"Well, it amounts to that," Swift told her steadfastly, for he knew what he meant to say, and was not to be deterred by the snubs and worse to which he was knowingly laying himself open.

"Pray how do you know what it amounts to?"

"On your side, at any rate, it amounts to an engagement; for you consider yourself bound."

"Upon my word!" cried Tiny hastily. "Do you mind telling me how you come to know so much about my affairs?"

"I am naturally interested in them after all these years."

"How very kind of you! How interested you were when I foolishly offered to tell you myself! So you have been talking me over with Herbert, have you?"

"We have spoken about you to-day for the first time; that is why I'm here."

Christina was white with anger.

"And I suppose," she sneered, "that you have told him things which I have forgotten, and which you might have forgotten as well!"

"I don't think you do suppose that," Swift said gently. "No, he merely told me about your engagement."

"Then why do you want me to tell you?"

"Because you alone can tell me what I most want to know."

"Oh, indeed!"

"Yes—whether you are happy!"

She had found her temper, which enabled her to put a keener edge on the words, "That, I should say, is not your business"; and she stared at Swift coldly where he stood, with his hands behind him, looking down upon her without wincing.

"I am not so sure," said he sturdily. "I loved you dearly; *I* could have made you happy."

"It is well you think so," was the best answer she could think of for that; and she did not think of it at once. "Do you know who he is?" she added later.

"Herbert told me. It seems you have tampered with a splendid chance."

"I have tampered with three. I shall jump at the next—if I get another."

"And if you don't?"

Involuntarily she drew a deep breath at the thought. Her head was lifted, and her blue eyes wandered over the yellow distance of the plains with the look of a prisoner coming back into the world.

"Nobody could blame him," she said at last, "and I should be rightly served."

Swift crouched in front of her, almost sitting on his heels to peer into her face.

"Tiny," he suddenly cried, "you don't love him one bit!"

"But I think he loves me," she answered, hanging her head, for he held her hand.

"Not as I do, Tiny! Never as I have done! I have loved you all the time, and never anyone but you. And you—you care for me best; I see it in your eyes; I feel it in your hand. Don't you think that you, too, may have loved me all the time?"

"If I have," she murmured, "it has been without knowing it."

It was without knowing it that she trod upon the truth. Their voices were trembling.

"Darling," he whispered, "this would be home to you. It's the same old Wallandoon. You love it, I know; and I think—you love——"

She snatched her hand from his, and sprang to her feet. He, too, rose astounded, gazing on every side to see who was coming. But the plain was flecked only with straggling sheep, bleating to the troughs. His gaze came back to the girl. Her straw hat sharply shadowed her face like a highwayman's mask, her blue eyes flashing in the midst of it, and her lips below parted in passion.

"You? I hate you! I *do* consider myself bound, and you would make me false—you would tempt me through my love for the bush, for this place—you coward!"

Swift reddened, and there was roughness in his answer:

"I can't stand this, even from you. I have heard that all women are unfair; you are, certainly. What you say about my tempting you is nonsense. You have shown me that you love me, and that you don't love the other man; you know you have. You have now to show whether you have the courage of your love—to give him up—to marry me."

This method must have had its attractions after another's; but it hurt, because Tiny was sensitive, with all her sins.

"You have spoken very cruelly," she faltered, delightfully forgetting how she had spoken herself. "I could not marry anyone who spoke to me like that!"

"Oh, forgive me!" he cried, covered with contrition in an instant. "I am a rough brute, but I promise——" He stopped, for her head had drooped, and she seemed to be crying. He stood away from her in his shame. "Yes, I am a rough brute," he repeated bitterly; "but, darling, you don't know how it roughens one, bossing the men!"

Still she hung her head, but within the widened shadow of her hat he saw her red mouth twitching at his clumsiness. Yet, when she raised her face, her smile astonished him, it was so timorous; and the wondrous shyness in her lovely eyes abashed him far more than her tears.

"I dare say—I need that!" he heard her whisper in spurts. "I think I should like—you—to boss—me—too."

These things and others were tersely told in a letter written in the hot blast of a north wind at Wallandoon, and delivered in London six weeks later, damp with the rain of early April. The letter arrived by the last post, and Ruth read it on the sofa in her husband's den, while Erskine paced up and down the room, listening to the sentences she read aloud, but saying little.

"So you see," said Ruth as she put the thin sheets together and replaced them in their envelope, "she accepted him before she knew of Lord Manister's engagement. *He* knew of it, and had undertaken to tell her, but that was only to give himself a last chance. Had she heard of it first he would never have spoken again."

"I question that," Erskine said thoughtfully. "He might not have spoken so soon; but his love would have proved stronger than his pride in the end. Yet I like him for his pride. That was what she needed, and what Manister lacked. It is very curious."

"I wonder if you really would like him," said Ruth, who no longer cared for the sound of Lord Manister's name. "I don't remember much about him, except that we all thought a good deal of him; but somehow I don't fancy he's your sort."

"I wasn't aware that I had a sort," Erskine said, smiling.

"Oh, but you have. *I* am not your sort. But Tiny was!"

He laughed heartily.

"Then we four have chosen sides most excellently! It is quite fatal to marry your own sort. Didn't you know that, my dear?"

"No, I didn't," said Ruth, watching him from the sofa; "but I am very glad to hear it, and I quite agree. You and Tiny, for instance, would have jeered at everything in life until you were left jeering at one another. Don't you think so?" she added wistfully, after a pause.

"I think you're an uncommonly shrewd little person," Erskine remarked, smiling down upon her kindly, so that her face shone with pleasure.

"Do you?" she said, as he helped her to rise. "You used to think me so dense when Tiny was here; and I dare say I was—beside Tiny."

"My dearest girl," said Erskine, taking his wife in his arms, and speaking in a troubled tone, "you have never said that sort of thing before, and I hope you never will again. Tiny was Tiny—our Tiny—but surely wisdom was not her strongest point? She amused us all because she wasn't quite like other people; but how often am I to tell you that I am thankful you are not like Tiny?"

"Ah, if you really were!" Ruth whispered on his shoulder.

"But I always was," he answered, kissing her; and they smiled at one another until the door was shut and Ruth had gone, for there was now between them an exceeding tenderness.

Ruth had left him her letter, so that he might read it for himself; but though he lit a pipe and sat down, it was some time before Erskine read anything. Had Ruth returned and asked him for his thoughts, he would have confessed that he was wondering whether Tiny's husband would understand the girl he had managed to tame; and whether he had a fine ear for a joke. As wondering would not tell him, he at length turned to the letter; and that did not tell him either; but before he turned the first of the many leaves, it was as though the child herself was beside him in the room.

The qualities she mentioned in her beloved were all of a serious character, and the praises she bestowed upon him, at her own expense, were a little tiresome to one who did not know the man. Erskine turned over with excusable impatience, and was rewarded on the next page by a sufficiently just summary of Lord Manister; even here, however, Tiny took occasion to be very hard on herself. She declared—possibly she would have said it in any case, but it happened to be true—that she had never loved Lord Manister. On the way she had ill-used him she harped no more; his own solution of his difficulties had, indeed, broken that string. But she spoke of her "temptation" (incidentally remarking that the hall windows haunted her still), and said she would perhaps have yielded to it outright but for her visit to Wallandoon before sailing for England; and that she would certainly have done so at the third asking had it not been for that stronger temptation to go back with Herbert to Australia. As it was, she had gone back fully determined to marry Lord Manister in the end. And if that decision had been furthered to the smallest extent by any sort of consideration for another, she did not say so; neither did she seek to defend her own behavior at any point, for this was not Tiny's way. However, with Jack she had burned to justify herself, because love puts an end to one's ways. She had longed to tell him everything with her own lips, and to have him forgive and excuse her on the spot. This she admitted. But she denied having known what her unreasonable longing really was. Did Ruth remember the "burning of the boats" at Cintra? Well, she had spoken the truth about Jack then; she had never "known" until the night of her last arrival at the station; she had never been quite miserable until the succeeding days. Reverting to Manister, she supposed the discovery of her departure the day after their interview—in which she had studiously refrained from revealing its imminence—had proved the last straw with him; she added that such a result had been vaguely in her mind at the time, but that she had never really admitted it among her hopes. Yet it seemed she had cured him just when she gave him up for incurable—and how thankful she was! A well-felt word about Lord Manister's future happiness and so on led her to her own; and Erskine slid his eye over that, but had it arrested by a loving little description of the old home to which she was coming back for good. It was a hot wind as she wrote, and the beginning of a word dried before she got to the end of it—so she affirmed. The roof was crackling, and the shadows in the yard were like tanks of ink. Out on the run the salt-bush still looked healthy after the rains. She had given up whim driving; the manager had put in his word. But she was taking long rides, all by herself; and the lonely grandeur of the bush appealed to her just as it had when she first came back to it nearly a year ago; and the deep sky and yellow distances and dull leaves were all her eyes required; and she thought this was the one place in the world where it would be easy to be good.

The letter came rather suddenly to its end. There were some very kind words about himself, which Erskine read more than once. Then he sat staring into the fire, until, by some fancy's trick, the red coals turned pale and took the shape of a girl's sweet face with blemishes that only made it sweeter, with dark hair, and generous lips, and eyes like her own Australian sky. And the eyes lightened with fun and with mischief, with recklessness, and bitterness, and temper; and in each light they were more lovable than before; but last of all they beamed clear and tranquil as the blue sea becalmed; and in their depths there shone a soul.

THE END.

Milton Keynes UK
Ingram Content Group UK Ltd.
UKHW011142220424
441551UK00007B/749